ENGLISH FOR ACADEMIC PURPOSES SERIES

General Editor: Vaughan James

EARTH SCIENCES

Christopher St J Yates

Cassell

Cassell Publishers Ltd
Artillery House
Artillery Row
London
SW1P 1RT

© Cassell Publishers Limited 1988

First published 1988

British Library Cataloguing in Publication Data

Yates, Christopher St. John
Earth sciences.—(English for academic
purposes).
Student's book
1. English language. For non-English
speaking students
I. Title. II.Series
428.2'4

ISBN 0 304 31517 6

A series designed and developed by Passim Ltd, Oxford, and Associates

Printed in England

Earth Sciences Teacher's Book 0 304 31518 4
Cassettes   0 304 31519 2

CONTENTS

INTRODUCTION

This course has three purposes. It is intended:
- to introduce you to the **contents** of Earth Sciences:
- to provide examples of authentic texts written in the **language** typical of the subject:
- to help you to practise the **skills** you will need in order to study the subject via English and to use it when you have learned it.

No knowledge of Earth Sciences is assumed, but if you work through the book carefully you will certainly learn a great deal about it. We do not set out to give comprehensive coverage, but the material does embrace most of the basic concepts. In this sense it is a basic textbook of Earth Sciences.

All the texts are taken from publications about Earth Sciences. They are not simplified for learners of English: the language you will encounter in them is exactly what you will meet in real life. We assume that you will have already taken a course of general English and are familiar with the main grammatical structures and much of the vocabulary of everyday use. There may be no such thing as Earth Sciences English, but there are a number of words and expressions commonly used in Earth Sciences contexts and there are a number of structures also in common use, and these have been isolated for you to practise. So in this sense, this is a textbook of English.

The most important aim of the course, however, is to help you to acquire and develop the skills you will need in order to learn your subject and, when you have finished the course, to use what you will have learned.

When you begin to study a new subject, you do so in two main ways: by **reading** and by **listening**. These are the major means of access to new knowledge and it is on these that we concentrate, via the **book** — for reading, and the **tapes** — for listening. In order to attack all these aims, we have divided each of the 15 units into 8 sections, closely related but each with a slightly different emphasis. Below we give a brief description of each section, so that at any point in any unit you will know exactly what you are expected to do and why you are doing it. The pattern is the same for all units.

A. UNDERSTANDING A PRINTED TEXT (1): In this section you are given a passage to read, usually including a diagram or table, to introduce the topic of the unit. You should first read it through, even if you do not understand it all, looking especially at the way it is set out in paragraphs, with side headings, marginal notes, captions, etc. This will give you a general idea of what it is about and how it is arranged. You will probably need to read it several times.

B. CHECK YOUR UNDERSTANDING: To help you to identify the most important points in the reading passage, a small number of questions are given, the answers to which you can look out for as you read. You could tackle them by jotting down a few notes and then turning your notes into complete answers, which your teacher will check. When you are clear about the general meaning of the passage, you can work through it in more detail with your dictionary. You should *always* have a dictionary handy and *never* be too proud (or too lazy!) to look things up.

C. INCREASE YOUR VOCABULARY: In this section you are asked to look at certain words which are used in the text, and there are several kinds of activity to help you remember them. Notice that they are not all new or technical terms; it is often familar words used in an unfamiliar way that will cause you trouble.

D. CHECK YOUR GRAMMAR: There are probably no new grammatical structures in the texts, but you may need reminding of some of them. The most important ones arising from the texts are revised and practised in this section.

E.UNDERSTANDING A LECTURE / H. UNDERSTANDING DISCOURSE: Sections A–D are all concerned with gaining access to new information through reading, but an important source of information is through listening — to lectures, talks, discussions, even simple conversations between fellow students — so sections E and H are both based on the recordings, to which you should listen (usually several times) before attempting to answer the questions or perform the activities given in your book. You will hear a variety of voices and accents, all speaking at the sort of speed that is customary in an English-speaking environment.

F. UNDERSTANDING A PRINTED TEXT (2) / G. CHECK YOUR UNDERSTANDING: These two sections are very similar to A and B, but the questions in section G are far more detailed and you will need to study the text very carefully in order to answer them.

Although we hope that you will enjoy working through this course, we do not expect you to find it easy. At various times you will probably start wondering how much you have been learning — or your teacher will want to find out what progress you are making. So after Units 5 and 10 we have included progress checks (not tests!) so that you can get a fairly clear idea of this. By the time you have completed Unit 15, you will be ready for anything!

Some of the texts are written in American English, which has some differences from British English, especially in spelling (e.g. *Br.* vapour, *Am.* vapor). You might find it useful to keep a running list of such examples. Remember that they are equally acceptable, but you should avoid mixing them in a single piece of writing.

Vaughan James   Oxford, 1988

1. What do you know about this topic? (oral)

English for Academic Purposes

THE EARTH

A. Understanding a printed text (1)

2. Surveying the contents

1.

The following text will introduce you to the topic of **the earth**. Look at the way it is divided into sections and paragraphs. Pay attention to the headings and notes in the margins, and to the illustrations and captions.

3. Scanning

Now look at these questions:

1. The text has two sections. What is each section about?
2. What shape did the Egyptians think the universe was?

3. What shape did the Greeks think the universe was?
4. Who made the most accurate measurement of the earth's radius?
5. What force is named as the reason for the earth's shape?

Read the passage through and find the answers to the questions. Remember, you do not have to understand every word to answer them.

Size

1 The ancient Egyptians saw the universe as a great box, with Egypt in the center of its long, narrow floor. The top of the box was the sky, from which lamps were suspended by means of ropes. These were the stars. Other lamps, which were carried in heavenly boats, traveled about the sky and appeared as planets. They thought the Milky Way was the equivalent of the Nile, and the regions through which it flowed were where dead Egyptians lived.

2 As time went on, people began to put together a remarkably accurate picture of the earth and the solar system. As early as the fifth century B.C., Parmenides declared that the earth was a sphere. It is probable that he realized this from listening to travelers. These discovered that, when they went north, a greater number of stars remained above the horizon all night (Fig. 1.1). They also realized that, when they went south, they could see other stars (for instance, Canopus, which can not be seen from Greece). The early travelers also reported that the length of the day changed with what we now call latitude. This was rather difficult to explain in terms of a flat earth.

3 In time, when the ancient Greeks accepted that the earth was round, attempts were made to estimate its size. Aristotle quotes 400,000 stadia for the circumference. This is much too big. He does not say where he got this figure from. Probably he took it from the earlier work of Eudoxus, a mathematician and astronomer. Archimedes later gave the circumference as 300,000 stadia. This is better, though still 20 percent in error.

4 Eratosthenes made the best of the early measurements of the earth's circumference. He worked in the great library at Alexandria. He knew that, at Syene, which was due south of Alexandria, the sun was directly overhead at midday on the first day of summer. On the first day of summer in 250 B.C., he carefully measured the extent to which the sun's rays slanted away from the vertical at midday in Alexandria. He found that this angle was $\frac{1}{50}$ of a complete circle, or a little over 7° (Fig. 1.2). Since the distance from Syene to Alexandria was 5,000 stadia, the circumference of the earth, corresponding to a full circle of 360°, must be 50 times 5,000, or 250,000 stadia.

The earth according to the ancient Egyptians

The ancient Greeks knew the earth was a sphere

How the earth's radius was first accurately determined

▼

5 How long is a stadium? There were several different stadia in use in the ancient world. Eratosthenes probably used the stadium of 517 ft. This means a circumference of 24,500 mi. This is not far from more recent calculations of 24,860 mi. In round numbers, the earth's radius is 4,000 mi, the same as 6,400 km.

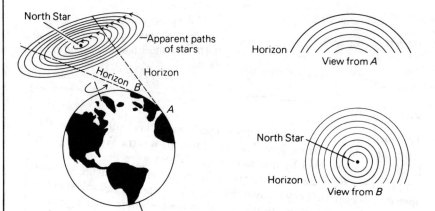

Fig. 1.1 At high latitudes more stars remain above the horizon all night than at low latitudes, evidence of the earth's sphericity.

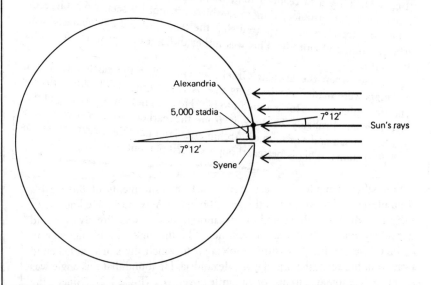

Fig. 1.2 How Eratosthenes determined the circumference of the earth.

Shape

6   Why is the earth round? Why does it not look like an egg or a pyramid?

7   We can understand the shape of the earth by considering the pressures beneath the earth's surface. Pressure in water is familiar enough: a dam must be much thicker at the bottom than at the top in order to withstand the greater pressure. A submarine can descend only a few hundred feet under the surface of the sea. Below that its hull will collapse. These forces are due to the weight of the overlying liquid. This in turn is a consequence of the earth's gravitational pull. With increasing distance below the surface of the earth, pressures quickly become enormous. No material can resist these pressures without flowing in response. This means that one part of the earth cannot project outward very much farther than other parts; if it did, the pressure under it would be greater than under surrounding regions. The rock beneath the bump would then flow out to the sides until the pressures were equalized.

8   Thus gravity is what gives the earth a spherical shape and keeps all parts of its surface the same distance from the center. Such minor irregularities as mountains and ocean basins do not greatly disturb the pressure balance, but no large protuberance can exist.

Gravity is the cause of the earth's spherical shape

B. Check your understanding

Now read the text carefully, looking up any new items in a dictionary or reference book. Then answer the following questions: *after reading!!*

1. Where was Egypt in the 'box'?   *centre of float*

2. What did the Milky Way correspond to?   *the Nile*

3. Where did Parmenides probably get his information?   *listening to travellers*

4. Who made the better estimate of the earth's circumference, Aristotle or Archimedes?   *Archimedes.*

5. Why was Syene important to Eratosthenes?   *sun directly overhead at mid-day on 1st of summer.*

6. How long was the stadium Eratosthenes used?   *517 ft*

7. What is the most recent calculation of the earth's circumference given in the text?   *24,860 mi*

8. What happens to a submarine that goes down too deep?   *Hull will collapse*

9. Why is a dam thicker at the bottom than at the top?   *great pressure*

10. Do mountains have any effect on the pressure balance?   *not greatly.*

Note: All the reading passages in this book have been taken from Beiser & Krauskopf, *Introduction to Earth Science*, McGraw-Hill, 1975. Some have been slightly adapted.

C. Increase your vocabulary

In this section you should use your dictionary to help you answer the questions about the text.

1. Look at the first paragraph and say what these words refer to:

- line 2: its ~ _box_
- line 2: which ~ _sky (top of box)_
- line 3: These ~ _lamps_
- line 5: They ~ _ancient Egyptian_
- line 6: which ~ _Milky Way_

2. Look at paragraph 2 and say what these words refer to:

- line 4: this ~ _earth is a sphere_
- line 6: They ~ _traveler_
- line 9: This ~ _length of day changes_

3. Look at paragraph 2 again. Using your dictionary, say what words or expressions in the text you could replace with:

- astonishingly ~ _remarkably_
- likely ~ _probable_
- find out ~ _discover_
- stay ~ _remain_

4. Look at paragraph 3 and say which words in the text have the same meaning as:

- very old ~ _ancient_
- try ~ _attempt_
- mistake ~ _error_

5. Look at paragraph 4. Using the information in the text, how much of the diagram below can you label? Try to do so without looking at the diagram in the reading text.

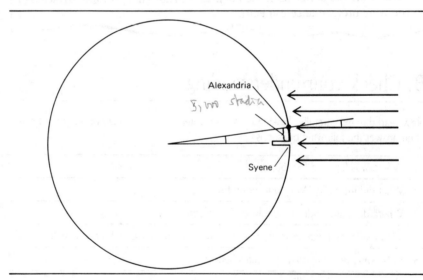

6. Now look at the second section of the text and try to explain the following words:

- pyramid
- pressure
- dam
- region
- protuberance

7. Varieties of English

Some of the words in this passage are spelt in the American way, which is slightly different from the spelling in British English. Two examples are given below; can you find any others? Start a running list and keep it up to date as you work through this book. Remember that neither version is 'right' or 'wrong', but you should be aware of the difference:

American English	British English
center	centre
traveled	travelled

D. Check your grammar

Do you remember?
Most people *think* that the earth is round.
Science *is taught* at most universities in the world.

---

1. Use the following verbs to complete the paragraph below:
be, rotate, wrinkle, warp, flatten, call, bulge, turn, exhibit, have

Although the earth _____ more nearly round than any other shape, it _____ not a perfect sphere. In fact the earth _____ slightly at the equator and _____ at the poles. For this reason it _____ much like a grapefruit. The total distortion _____ not great. The effect _____ *centrifugal distortion*, since the equatorial regions _____ furthest from the centre.

The earth _____ about 0.34 percent away from being a perfect sphere. Venus, which _____ very slowly, _____ very little centrifugal distortion; Jupiter, Saturn and Uranus, all of which _____ rapidly on their axes, _____distortions of 6.2, 9.6 and 6 percent, respectively.

The overall flattening of the earth _____ not its only deviation in shape from a perfect sphere. Our planet _____ and its skin _____ into mountains and valleys both above and below sea level.

Do you remember?
The astronomer Tycho Brahe *built* an observatory in Denmark.
His instruments *were made* as precise and rigid as possible.

---

2. Now write the following sentences out in full, like this:

Tycho/eyesight/patience/and/exceptional . . . . (possess)
Tycho possessed exceptional eyesight and patience.

- Tycho/observatory/Denmark/in/an. . . . (construct)

- measurements/these/thousands/he/of/make/to/instruments . . . . (use)

- assistant/Johannes Kepler/the . . . . (call)

- invention/Tycho/the/telescope/of/before/the . . . . (live)

- astronomer/better-known/a/Kepler/than/master/his . . . . (become)

- precision/his/instruments/great/with . . . . (make)

- 1601/in/Tycho . . . . (die)

- celestial angles/despite/better/disadvantage/to/one-hundredth of a degree/than/this/ he . . . . (determine)

- labour/his/much/it/a/which/life/was/of . . . . (occupy)

- peculiar theory/a/superb/body/the/of/data/solar system/he/and/a/of/an assistant . . . . (leave behind)

---

3. Now arrange the sentences you have made into a single paragraph. Make sure that the order you arrange the sentences in makes sense!

E. Understanding a lecture

1. You are now going to hear part of a lecture, divided into short sections to help you understand it. As you listen, answer the following questions:

Section 1————————————————————————————————————

- The lecturer says one word is not adequate to describe the earth's shape. What is that word?
- Name one of the questions the lecturer is going to discuss.

Section 2————————————————————————————————————

- Look at the overhead transparency below. Label the three models using the information the lecturer has given you.

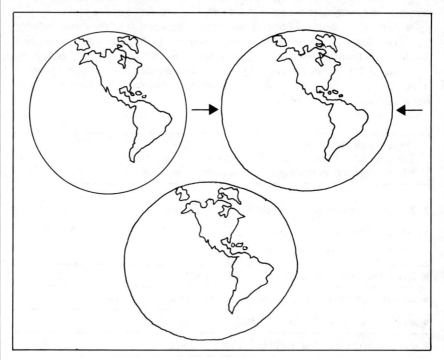

- Are these three models the only ones used to describe the earth's shape?

Section 3————————————————————————————————————

- Write down the term the lecturer wants you to note.
- Who first computed the earth in terms of an oblate spheroid?

Section 4————————————————————————————————————

- What terms does the lecturer use to describe 'the bits that stick out' and the 'dents'.
- Which, if any, of the three models is 100% accurate?

2. Now wind the tape back to the beginning of the lecture and listen to it again. This time, instead of answering questions, take notes. The questions you have already answered will help you do this. When you have listened to the whole of the lecture, you will be asked to make a short oral summary of it, using your notes as a guide. So make sure you note down the most important points.

F. Understanding a printed text (2)

Read the following text carefully, looking up anything you do not understand.

Latitude and Longitude

1   Locations on the earth's surface are specified in terms of the earth's axis of rotation. A *great circle* is any circle on the earth's surface whose center is the earth's center. The *equator* is a great circle midway between the North and South Poles (Fig. 1.13). A *meridian* is a great circle that passes through both poles, and it forms a right angle with the equator. The *prime meridian* passes through Greenwich, England. The *longitude* of a point on the earth's surface is the angular distance between a meridian through this point and the prime meridian; the prime meridian is assigned the longitude 0°, and longitudes are given in degrees east or west of the prime meridian. Thus a longitude of 60°W identifies a meridian 60° west of the prime meridian.

Longitude measures angular distance east or west of the prime meridian through Greenwich

2.   The *latitude* of a point on the earth's surface is the angle between a line drawn from the earth's center to it and another line drawn from the center to a point on the equator on the same meridian. Thus the latitude of the North Pole is 90°N, that of the South Pole is 90°S, and that of the equator itself is just 0°. A latitude of 60°N identifies a circle 60° north of the equator. Degrees of latitude and longitude are further divided into *minutes* [1° = 60 minutes (60′)], and minutes are further divided into *seconds* [1′ = 60 seconds (60″)]. A *nautical mile* is equal to a minute of latitude, and is 6,080 ft in length. (A statute mile, used on land, is 5,280 ft in length.) Because of the way they are defined, parallels of latitude are equally spaced everywhere

Latitude measures angular distance north or south of the equator

A nautical mile is a minute of latitude

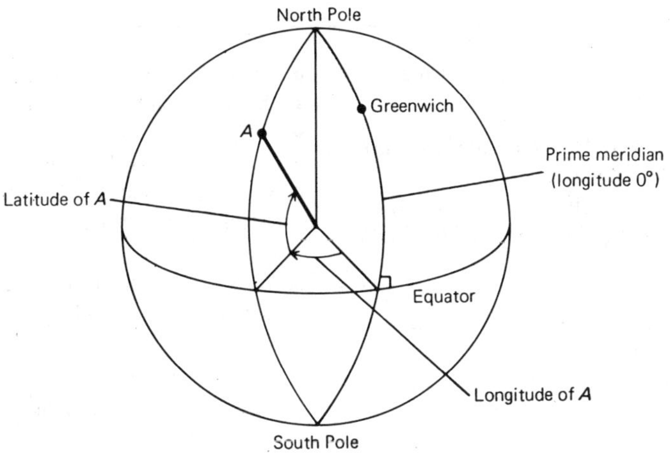

Fig. 1.13 How latitude and longitude are defined.

(hence the usefulness of the nautical mile), but meridians of longitude converge at the poles.

3 On December 22, the shortest day of the year in the Northern Hemisphere, the 23.5° tilt of the earth's axis means that no sunlight reaches any point within 23.5° from the North Pole. The *Arctic Circle* is the boundary of this region of darkness (Fig. 1.14). On the same day, which is the longest day of the year in the Southern Hemisphere, there are 24 h of daylight at all points within 23.5° of the South Pole, and the *Antarctic Circle* is the boundary of this region of daylight. On June 22 the situations in the two hemispheres are reversed.

4 The *Tropic of Cancer* is the most northerly latitude in the Northern Hemisphere at which the sun is ever directly overhead at noon. The *Tropic of Capricorn* is the corresponding latitude in the Southern Hemisphere. On June 22, when the North Pole is tilted closest to the sun and which is hence the day of maximum sunlight in the Northern Hemisphere, the noon sun is directly overhead 23.5° north of the equator; hence the latitude of the Tropic of Cancer is 23.5° N. Similarly the latitude of the Tropic of Capricorn is 23.5° S; the South Pole is tilted closest to the sun on December 22, when the noon sun is directly overhead at this latitude.

G. Check your understanding

1. What do the following stand for?

°	S	"	W	h
N		ft	E	Fig.

2. Find the terms in the text which describe the following:

- The name of the meridian which passes through Greenwich.
- A great circle that is drawn midway between the North Pole and the South Pole.
- The name of the most southerly latitude above which the sun is directly overhead at 12 noon.
- The name of that latitude's equivalent in the Northern Hemisphere.

- A mile that is 6,080 ft long.
- The point that has a latitude of 90°N.
- The point that has a latitude of 90°S.
- A mile that is used on land.
- Any circle on the earth's surface whose centre is the earth's centre.

3. These words can all be explained in simpler, more everyday language. Can you do that?

- location
- rotation
- assign
- further

H. Understanding discourse

1. Listen to the conversation between some students and their tutor. The students should have read the same text that you have just read. The tutor is checking whether they have understood or not. Listen to them talking and say whether the students have answered correctly or incorrectly.

If the answer is correct, put a tick in the box ☑

If it is wrong, put a cross in the box ☒

1. ☐
2. ☐
3. ☐
4. ☐
5. ☐

2. Did you notice in that conversation how the tutor asked his questions? If you do not understand something, you can ask for an explanation in a number of ways. Look at this table:

(Excuse me) (I'm sorry, but)	can you could you	explain . . . . tell me a bit more about	
	I don't really understand . . . . could you (possibly/please) repeat		that last bit . . . . what you just said . . . .

Imagine you do not understand the following terms. Ask each other for an explanation:

- Tropic of Cancer
- Tropic of Capricorn
- South Pole
- North Pole
- Equator

ENERGY

A. Understanding a printed text (1)

The following text will introduce you to the topics of **work** and **energy**. Look at the way it is divided into sections and paragraphs. Pay attention to the headings and notes in the margins, and to the illustrations and captions.

Now look at these questions:

1. The text has two sections. What is each section about?
2. What rule is given for defining *work*?

3. What two systems of units are mentioned in the first section?
4. How many kinds of energy are mentioned in the text?
5. How is energy defined?

Read the passage through and find the answers to the questions. Remember, you do not have to understand every word to answer them.

ENERGY

1 Usually we associate the word *energy* with activity or motion: a falling stone possesses energy, an energetic person is constantly doing things. Sometimes, though, we speak of certain foods as being rich in energy or of the earth as receiving radiant energy from the sun. What is it that a piece of pie and a falling stone have in common? The answer is, they both possess the ability to accomplish change, whether directly as in the case of the stone, or indirectly as in the case of the pie. In order to establish how energy and change are related, we begin by defining the physical quantity called *work*.

Work

2 Changes that occur in the physical world are invariably the result of forces. Forces are needed to pick things up, to move things from one place to another, to squeeze things, to stretch things, and so on. However, not all forces produce changes, and it is the distinction between forces that accomplish change and those that do not that is central to the idea of work.

3 If we push against a stone wall, nothing happens. We have applied a force, but the wall has not yielded and shows no effects. However, if we apply the same force to a stone, the stone flies through the air for some distance (Fig. 2.1). Now something has been accomplished as the result of our push. The basic difference between the two situations is that, in the first case, the wall did not move, but in the second, the stone was moving during the time the force was applied. It was the displacement of the body while the force acted upon it that was responsible for the difference in the two results.

4 As a general rule, whenever a force produces effects such as motion or distortion in an object, a displacement of some kind accompanies the application of the force. This concept is made specific by defining the work done by a force as the product of the force and the distance through which it acts. If the distance is zero, no work is done by the force, no matter how great it is. And even if something moves through a distance, work is not done on it unless a force was acting.

Work equals force times displacement

5 In the British system of units, the unit of work is the *foot-pound*. One foot-pound is the amount of work done by a force of one pound that acts through a distance of one foot. In the metric system, the unit of work is the *joule* (J), where 1 J is equal to 0.738 ft-lb.

Units of work

6 The rate at which work is being done by some agency is called *power*. The more powerful an engine is, the more work it can perform in a certain length of time. The metric unit of power is the *watt* (W), where one watt is equal to one joule per second. The *horsepower* (hp) is the customary unit of power in engineering: 1 hp equals 746 W or 550 ft-lb/s.

Power is the rate of doing work

No work done

Work done

Fig. 2.1 The work done by a force on a body is the product of the force and the distance through which the body moves while the force acts upon it. For a force to do work on a body, the body must undergo a displacement while the force acts on it. No work is done by pushing against a rigid wall.

Energy

7 Energy may be thought of as that property of something which enables it to do work. When we say that something possesses energy, we suggest that it is capable in some way of exerting a force on something else and performing work on it. When work is done on something, on the other hand, energy has been added to it. Energy is measured in the same units as those of work, the foot-pound and the joule.

8 Energy occurs in several forms. A familiar example is the energy a moving body possesses by virtue of its motion. Every moving object has the capacity to do work. By striking another object that is free to move, the moving object can exert a force and cause the second object to shift its position. It is not necessary that the moving object actually do work; it may keep on moving, or friction may slowly bring it to a stop. But while it is moving, it has the *capacity* for doing work. It is this specific property that defines energy, since energy means the ability to do work, and so all moving things have energy by virtue of their motion. This type of energy is called *kinetic energy.*

Energy is the capacity to do work; that is, to produce change

Kinetic energy is energy of motion

▼

Potential energy is energy of position

9   The statement that energy is the capacity something has to do work is not restricted to kinetic energy but is perfectly general. Many objects possess energy because of their *position*. Consider a pile driver, a simple machine that lifts a heavy weight (the "hammer") and allows it to fall on the head of a pile, thereby driving the pile into the ground. When the hammer has been lifted to the top, it has only to be released to fall and do work on the pile. The capacity for doing work is present in the hammer as soon as it has been lifted, simply because of its position several feet above the ground. The actual work on the pile is done at the expense of kinetic energy gained during the hammer's fall, but the capacity for working is present before the fall starts. Energy of this sort, depending merely on the position of an object, is called *potential energy*.

10   Examples of potential energy are everywhere. A book on a table has potential energy, since it can fall to the floor; a skier at the top of a slope, water at the brink of a cataract, a car at the top of a hill, anything capable of moving toward the earth under the influence of gravity has energy because of its position. Nor is the earth's gravity necessary: a planet has potential energy with respect to the sun, since it can do work in falling toward the sun; a nail placed near a magnet has potential energy, because it can do work in moving to the magnet.

11   Nearly all familiar mechanical processes actually consist of interchanges of energy among its kinetic and potential forms and work. Thus when the car of Fig. 2.2 drives to the top of a hill, its engine must do work in order to raise the car. At the top, the car has an amount of potential energy equal to the work done in getting it up there (neglecting friction). If the engine is turned off, the car can still coast down the hill, and its kinetic energy at the bottom of the hill will be the same as its potential energy at the top.

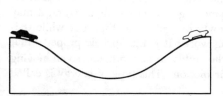

Fig. 2.2   Conservation of energy. In the absence of friction, a car can coast from the top of one hill into a valley and then up to the top of another hill of the same height as the first. In doing this the initial potential energy of the car is converted into kinetic energy as it goes downhill, and this kinetic energy then turns into potential energy as it climbs the next hill.

B. Check your understanding

Now read the text carefully, looking up any new items in a dictionary or reference book. Then answer the following questions:

1. What is the first kind of energy mentioned in the text?

2. Why are forces needed?

3. What paragraph does Fig. 2.1 refer to?

4. What usually accompanies the application of force?

5. What is *power*?

6. What does hp stand for?

7. What does the word *capacity* mean?

8. How is *kinetic energy* defined?

9. The writer uses the example of a "pile driver". What is he illustrating with this example?

10. What does Fig. 2.2 illustrate?

C. Increase your vocabulary

In this section you should use your dictionary to help you answer the questions about the text.

1. Look at paragraph 1 again:

- What is an everyday word for 'motion'?
- Which word is used to mean 'has' or 'owns'?
- Which expression could you replace with 'share'?

2. Now look at paragraph 2:

- What word could you replace with 'always'?
- What expression has the same meaning as 'etc'?
- Can you explain the word 'distinction'?

3. Using words from paragraphs 3–6, can you complete the following statements?

- When you get into a bath, you _____ some of the water.
- The Greeks and ancient Egyptians had a different _____ of the shape of the earth.
- A large engine can _____ more work than a small one.
- When you kick a football you _____ force.

- A joule is a unit used to measure the _____ of work done.

4. Now look at paragraphs 7 and 8 and say which words have the same meaning as:

- can
- continue
- hitting
- kind *or* sort of
- movement

5. Now look at paragraph 9 and say which words have the opposite meaning to:

- held on to
- put down
- complicated
- absent
- lost

6. Now look at these definitions. Which words in the last three paragraphs correspond to the definitions?

- paying no attention to; ignoring
- well-known

- a small, pointed piece of metal used, for example, to join pieces of wood together
- one of the heavenly bodies that move round the sun
- a large, steep waterfall

D. Check your grammar

EXPRESSING CONDITIONS

> **Do you remember?**
> If we *push* against a stone wall, nothing *happens*.
> If you *drop* a glass on a stone floor, it *will break*.

1. Take one clause from each of the two columns below to make one sentence. Make sure your sentences make sense!

- If you don't eat,
- If a stone is thrown,
- If you drive carelessly,
- If you don't study,
- You'll get run over,
- If you eat a piece of pie,
- No work is done by the force,
- Nothing happens,
- If an object is moving,
- If it is released,
- A car won't go,

it has the capacity for doing work
a change is accomplished
if you don't start the engine
if you cross the road here
you'll crash
if you push against a house
you'll starve
the hammer will drive the pile into the ground
if the distance is zero
work is done
you'll fail your exam

> **Do you remember?**
> If our oil *ran out* tomorrow, my country *would lose* most of its energy.

2. Now say what you think would be the result if the circumstances below actually happened. Complete the sentences, giving your own opinion:

Example:
No/radiant/energy
If there was no radiant energy, ...

- My country/have/oil
- World's population/double/tomorrow
- World/have/no coal
- No/forces/in/world

- No/nuclear industry
- We/have/no electricity
- My car/not start
- Lose/my notes
- No library/in/university
- I/have/the chance

> **Do you remember?**
> If I *had not chosen* earth sciences, I *would have studied* physics instead.

3. Use the notes below to make complete sentences on the above model.

- Fail/my/entrance exam,
- I/be/ancient Egyptian,
- Saudi Arabia/not discover/oil,

- This university/not found,
- People/not discover/fire,

E. Understanding a lecture

1. You are now going to hear part of a lecture. The lecture will be divided into short sections to help you understand it. Here is the first section. Are you ready?

Section 1

- Is this the first lecture the speaker has given? How do you know?
- What is the subject of today's lecture?
- What example does the lecturer give to illustrate his point?
- What is a 'filament'?

Section 2

Below you can see the diagram on the overhead projector. Label the diagram according to the information given by the lecturer.

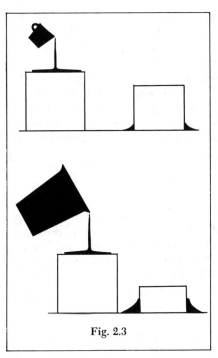

Fig. 2.3

Section 3

- What does F stand for?
- What does the lecturer say is a better word for 'way'?
- Using the diagram below and the information given by the lecturer, can you explain Fig. 2.4?

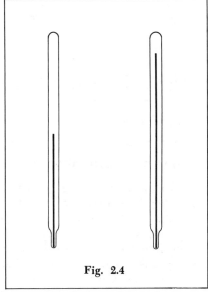

Fig. 2.4

Section 4

- What are the two scales for measuring temperature?
- Using the information the lecturer gives you, label as much of the diagram below as you can.

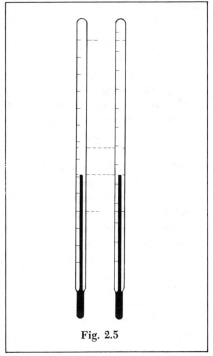

Fig. 2.5

15

2. Now wind the cassette back to the beginning of the lecture and listen to it again. This time, instead of answering questions, take notes. The questions you have already answered will help you do this. When you have listened to the whole of the lecture, you will be asked to make a short oral summary of the lecture you have heard. So make sure you note down the most important points of the lecture.

3. You should also write a summary of the lecture, based on your notes.

F. Understanding a printed text (2)

Read the following text carefully, looking up anything you do not understand.

Energy and Civilization

1   Almost all the energy available to us on the earth today has come ultimately from a single source—the sun. Light and heat reach us directly from the sun; food and wood owe their chemical energy to sunlight falling on plants; water power exists because the sun's heat evaporates water constantly from the oceans. The fossil fuels coal, oil, and natural gas were formed from plants and animals that lived and stored energy derived from sunlight millions of years ago.

2   Modern civilization owes its spectacular development in large measure to the discovery of vast sources of energy and to the development of new methods for storing and transforming it. Within less than 200 years man has learned to convert the chemical energy of coal, oil, and natural gas into mechanical energy, to store chemical energy in explosives, to get electrical energy from moving water, and to use electrical energy for heating, lighting, mechanical work, and communication. In the development of nuclear reactors a new energy source has been tapped—the energy stored in the interior of atoms. Other possible sources, still being explored, are the energy of tides and radiant energy direct from the sun.

3   The relative importance of the main energy sources of the past and present are shown in Fig. 2.6. It is evident how rapidly man's use of energy has grown in the last few decades. The chief reason is the increase in average energy use per person. A century ago, the rise of the industrial revolution led to the use of about 300 million J per person per day in the more advanced countries. Today the number of people who share the benefits of industrialization is much greater and they each tend to use more energy as well: in the United States, the energy used per person per day is three times the above figure. In fact, the United States, with 6 percent of the world's population, uses 35 percent of its energy.

4   Not all of the energy consumed today goes into manufacturing, transportation, lighting, space heating, and other traditional applications—more and more is being used to produce the artificial fertilizers needed by modern agriculture. This brings us to the aptly named population explosion: as discussed at the end of Chap. 11, the world's population will double in the next 30 years or so. To double food production is certainly possible, but only by the heavy use of fertilizers which will require disproportionately large amounts of energy. It is impossible to add substantially to the supply of food without first adding more substantially still to the energy supply. What will happen if the population continues to increase past the doubling that is in sight is not reassuring to contemplate.

The sun is the source of most of the energy available on the earth's surface

Much more energy is being used per person today than in the past

Population growth will greatly increase energy needs

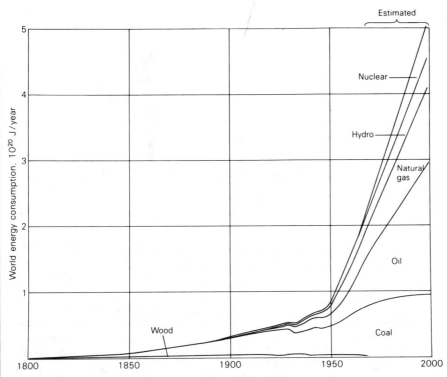

Fig. 2.6 World energy sources and consumption.

5   Clearly it is not possible to project present trends of energy demand very far ahead. On the supply side, the fossil fuels that today provide about 98 percent of man's energy will sooner or later be exhausted. Natural gas will be the first fossil fuel to run out, followed soon afterward by oil. Coal reserves are much greater, and ought to last at least another century. Nuclear fuels, too, are sufficient for another century or more.   And if practical methods for utilizing thermonuclear energy (the source of the sun's energy, as described in Chap. 13) are devised, the energy reserves available to man will be virtually unlimited. Though fossil fuels must inevitably diminish in importance, there seems to be no basic reason why other sources of energy cannot take their place.

Energy from fossil fuels will ultimately be replaced by nuclear and thermonuclear energy

6   However, despite the probable presence of adequate fuel of one kind or another, the current rate of increase of energy consumption cannot continue for very much longer. What stands in the way is the intrinsic inefficiency of all methods of converting heat into mechanical energy; electrical energy is included here, since it is produced by using mechanical energy to power generators. The inefficiency is not due to poor machinery but to the laws of thermodynamics—some heat *must* be wasted in every heat engine (Fig. 2.7). Even nuclear energy is inefficient, because it is turned into heat in a reactor and this heat is then used to operate a steam turbine which is connected to an electric generator. The conversion of heat into mechanical energy cannot be more than partly efficient, and some heat must be given off to the outside world.

Transforming heat into other forms of energy is always inefficient

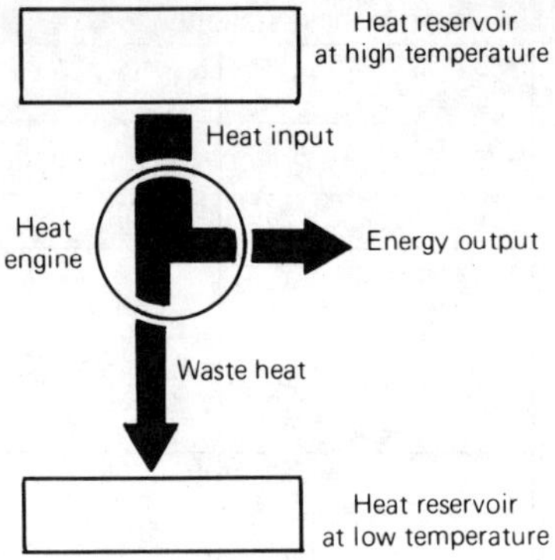

Fig. 2.7 A heat engine is a device that converts some of the heat flowing from a hot reservoir to a cold one into mechanical energy. Even an engine with the highest theoretically possible efficiency cannot make use of all of its heat input.

As energy consumption increases, the disposal of waste heat becomes more difficult

7   Even today the disposal of waste heat from power plants is a problem in the heavily industrialized parts of the world. Generating plants in the United States already use about 10 percent of the flow of all the rivers and streams of the country for cooling purposes. There are likely to be serious biological consequences if the scale of heating of inland waters rises much further, and if waste heat is instead discharged into the atmosphere with the help of cooling towers, the weather and climate of the region involved may be changed in a perhaps harmful way. Although the oceans can safely absorb much waste heat, locating power plants exclusively on their shores poses the question of transmitting the energy they produce for thousands of miles inland.

8   Nevertheless it seems clear that a considerable further increase in energy consumption is possible without undue environmental damage provided care is used. It also seems clear that no increase is possible which can keep up for much longer with both the current rise in worldwide living standards and the current rise in world population. The laws of thermodynamics are not subject to repeal, and a future energy crisis will represent a social failure, not a technological one.

G. Check your understanding

1. Find the terms in the text which describe the following:

- coal, oil and natural gas.
- the number of people in the world.
- something made by man; not natural.
- farming

- derive
- consume
- substantially
- contemplate
- sufficient
- utilize

2. These words can be explained in simpler, more everyday language. Can you do that?

3. Now look at these statements. Using the information in the text, say if they are correct or incorrect.

● We have water power because sunlight gives water chemical energy.	☐
● Animals and plants are the origin of fossil fuels.	☐
● Man makes considerable use of radiant energy today.	☐
● The United States uses more than half the world's energy.	☐
● The amount of energy used in agriculture is increasing.	☐
● We cannot double food production in the next 30 years.	☐
● The writer is not worried about the population increase.	☐
● The three fossil fuels will last another 100 years.	☐
● The writer does not believe the fossil fuels can be replaced.	☐
● The writer thinks thermonuclear energy will make no difference to our supply of energy.	☐

4. Now look at the last three paragraphs of the text. Summarise in your own words what the writer sees as problematic. First discuss what you think the main problems are, and then write your summary.

H. Understanding discourse

A lecturer is giving the title for an essay to be written during the coming week. He is also giving the main points that must be covered. Listen to what he says and note down what you must do.

_____

_____

_____

_____

_____

_____

_____

_____

MATTER

A. Understanding a printed text (1)

The following text will introduce you to the topic of **matter**. Look at the way it is divided into sections and paragraphs. Pay attention to the headings and notes in the margins, and to the illustration and caption.

Now look at these questions:

1. What is this text about?
2. In the first section (paragraphs 2–5) there are 4 key words. What are they?

3. To which paragraph does Fig. 2.8 refer?
4. There are 3 key words in the second section (paragraphs 6–8). What are they?

Read the passage through and find the answers to the questions. Remember, you do not have to understand every word to answer them.

MATTER

1 Suppose there were no limit to the power of our microscopes, so that we could examine a drop of water under stronger and stronger lenses indefinitely. What sort of microscopic world would we discover when the drop was enlarged, say, a million times? Would we still see structureless, transparent, liquid water? Or would we perhaps see distinct particles, the building blocks, as it were, of the water that to our unaided senses is a completely uniform substance? Long ago people began to suspect that matter, despite its appearance of being continuous, actually possesses a definite structure on a microscopic level. This suspicion did not take on a more concrete form until early in the last century. Since then the existence of atoms and molecules, the ultimate particles of matter in its common forms, has been amply demonstrated, and their own ultimate particles have been identified and studied as well.

Elements and Compounds

Elements are the basic ingredients of ordinary matter

2 *Elements* are substances that cannot be decomposed or transformed into one another by ordinary chemical or physical means. The earth contains only a limited number of elements, and all other materials consist of two or more of them combined in various ways. Of the 105 known elements (not all found on the earth), 11 are gases, 2 are liquids, and the rest are solids at room temperature and atmospheric pressure. Hydrogen, oxygen, chlorine, and neon are familiar gaseous elements; bromine and mercury are the two liquids; iron, zinc, tin, aluminum, copper, lead, silver, gold, carbon, and sulfur are among the solid elements.

Two or more elements may combine to form a compound with characteristic properties of its own

3 Some materials consist of two or more elements united in a *compound;* water is a compound of the elements hydrogen and oxygen. The elements in a compound are combined in definite, invariable proportions to form a new substance with characteristic properties of its own. In water, every gram of oxygen is combined with precisely 0.126 g of hydrogen, and it is a liquid at room temperature whereas hydrogen and oxygen are gases. Other materials consist of mixtures of elements or of compounds in which the separate substances do not lose their identities as they do in the case of a compound, and can be present in variable proportions.

4   The ultimate particles of an element are called *atoms*. A *molecule* is a group of atoms that stick together tightly enough to act as a unit. Many elemental gases consist of molecules instead of individual atoms. Thus gaseous oxygen contains molecules each of which is a pair of oxygen atoms bound together by forces whose nature we shall explore shortly. Other elemental gases, for instance helium and neon, consist of individual atoms. Most elemental solids and liquids are assemblies of individual atoms.

5   Many compounds consist of molecules. The molecules of a compound have specific compositions and structures, as Fig. 2.8 shows. Each water molecule contains two hydrogen atoms and one oxygen atom with the hydrogen atoms 105° apart, for example, while each ammonia molecule contains three hydrogen atoms 107.5° apart.

Molecule	Formula	Structure
Oxygen	O_2	
Carbon dioxide	CO_2	
Water	H_2O	
Ammonia	NH_3	

Fig. 2.8   Structures of several common molecules.

Chemical Symbols

6   By convention an atom of an element is represented by an abbreviation of the element's name. For many elements the first letter is used; an atom of oxygen is O, an atom of hydrogen H, an atom of carbon C. When the names of two elements begin with the same letter, two letters are used in the abbreviation for one or both: Cl stands for an atom of chlorine, He for helium, Zn for zinc. For some elements abbreviations of Latin names are used: a copper atom is Cu (cuprum), an iron atom Fe (ferrum), a mercury atom Hg (hydrargyrum). These abbreviations are called the *symbols* of the elements.

7   Two or more atoms joined to form a molecule are represented by writing their symbols side by side: a carbon monoxide molecule is CO, a zinc sulfide molecule ZnS, a mercuric oxide molecule HgO. When a molecule contains two or more atoms of the same kind, a subscript indicates the number present: the familiar expression H_2O means that a molecule of water contains two H atoms and one O atom; a molecule of oxygen, containing two O atoms, is written O_2; a molecule of carbon tetrachloride (CCl_4) contains one C atom and four Cl atoms; a molecule of nitrogen pentoxide (N_2O_5) contains two N (nitrogen) atoms and five O atoms. Each subscript applies only to the symbol immediately before it. These expressions for molecules are called *formulas*.

8   As a shorthand method of expressing the results of a chemical change, the formulas of the substances involved can be combined into a *chemical equation*. An equation includes the formulas of all the substances entering the reaction on the left-hand side with the formulas of all the products on the right-hand side. The formulas may be written in any order and are connected by + signs; between the two sides of the equation is placed an arrow. Thus, when carbon burns, the two substances that react are carbon (C) and oxygen (O_2), and the only product is carbon dioxide (CO_2):

$$C + O_2 \longrightarrow CO_2$$

This equation means, in words: "carbon reacts with oxygen to form carbon dioxide."

B. Check your understanding

Now read the text carefully, looking up any new items in a dictionary or reference book. Then answer the following questions:

1. What world is the writer talking about in the first paragraph?

2. What has been proved to exist over the last century?

3. How many known elements are there?

4. What kinds of elements are there?

5. What kinds of element are copper, mercury and chlorine?

6. What is a compound?

7. Do the elements of a compound change?

8. What is the difference between an atom and a molecule?

9. What is a symbol of an element?

10. Give an example of a chemical equation.

C. Increase your vocabulary

In this section you should use your dictionary to help you answer the questions about the text.

1. Look at paragraph 1 and say which words are used to mean:

- a piece of glass through which you look in cameras and other instruments
- to make bigger
- which can be seen through
- fully

2. Now look at paragraphs 2 and 3 and say which words have the opposite meaning to:

- unusual
- separate
- changing
- inexactly

3. Now look at paragraph 4 and say which words in the text you could replace with:

- closely
- so
- look into
- for example
- groupings

4. Now look at the second section, paragraphs 6–8. Can you explain the following words:

- abbreviation
- subscript
- formula

5. Express the following in words:

- ( )
- +
- →

6. Can you explain what the following are? Try not to look back at the text when you explain!

1.	2.	3.	4.
C	Ammonia	O_2	

D. Check your grammar

WRITING SENTENCES

Do you remember?
Some verbs in English are followed by the infinitive, 'to':
I *want to finish* my essay today.

Others are followed by the -ing form:
I *enjoy playing* football.

Verbs followed by a particle like 'in', 'from', etc. are followed by the -ing form:
He *insisted on going* to a film last night.

Some verbs can take both 'to' and -ing, but their meaning sometimes changes:
He *remembered* (= did not forget) *to bring* his books.
I *remember* (= recall) *meeting* his brother last year.

---

1. Complete the following sentences:

- He suggested (watch) _____ the football match on Saturday.
- I didn't stop (work) _____ until midnight last night.
- I'm sorry, I've forgotten (bring) _____ my essay.
- What models do we use (describe) _____ the earth?
- You must avoid (spill) _____ that chemical on your hands.
- Try (understand) _____ what I am saying.
- Try (look) _____ that word up in the dictionary.
- Would you mind (explain) _____ that again?
- The lecturer began (talk) _____ about atomic and molecular structure.
- Tomorrow I intend (discuss) _____ liquids and solids with you.
- Sickness prevented him from (attend) _____ the tutorial.
- I am looking forward to (study) _____ earth sciences.

WRITING PARAGRAPHS

2. Match the following clauses together, using *and*, *but*, *when*, *after*, *so* and *because*:

- the next evening he needed them
- he arrived at the canteen
- this did not please Andrew very much
- last night Andrew lent Robert his lecture notes
- Andrew needed his notes immediately
- he had waited for an hour

Robert could not attend
Robert finally arrived
he went to the canteen to look for Robert
Robert had not returned them
Robert was not there
he decided to wait

3. Now arrange your sentences into a sensible paragraph.

E. Understanding a lecture

You are now going to hear part of a lecture on gases, liquids and solids. The lecture will be divided into short sections to help you understand it. As you listen, answer the following questions:

Section 1 ———————————————

- How does the lecturer describe gases, liquids and solids?
- Is this statement correct or incorrect?

    The lecturer is not going to talk about atomic and molecular structure. ☐

Section 2 ———————————————

- Is this statement correct or incorrect?

    A gas consists mainly of molecules. ☐

- Complete the following statement correctly:

    When one molecule collides with another,
    there is no change. ☐

    the molecule only changes direction. ☐

    the molecule only changes speed. ☐

    the molecule changes both speed and direction. ☐

- To describe the way molecules behave, the lecturer gives two examples. What are they?

Section 3 ———————————————

- Is this statement correct or incorrect?

    A molecule can never stop moving. ☐

- Match these clauses according to the information given in the lecture:

    if a molecule's speed becomes greater than the average

    new collisions will set it in motion

    successive collisions will slow it down

- if a series of collisions brings it momentarily to a stop
- Complete the following sentence about the behaviour of molecules in a gas:

  There is no order in the _____, no uniformity of _____ or _____.

- The lecturer says two statements can be made about the behaviour of molecules. What are they?

Section 4

- Two reasons are given for the fact that gas can leak through small openings. What are they?

- Why can a gas be easily compressed?
- The lecturer says that gases can mix easily with one another and have a low density. What does he say the reason for this is?

Now write a summary of the lecture. You can listen again and make notes. The questions you have already answered will help you write the summary.

F. Understanding a printed text (2)

Read the following text, looking up anything you do not understand.

BOILING AND MELTING

1 The individual particles of every body of matter, whether a gas, a liquid, or a solid, are in constant, random motion. The total kinetic energy of this motion constitutes the *internal energy* of the body. When heat is added to the body, its internal energy increases; when the body loses heat, its internal energy decreases. Thus heat can be regarded as internal energy in transit.

Internal energy and heat

2 The temperature of a body of matter is a measure of the average kinetic energy of each of its particles. When we add heat to a pint of water, the water molecules share in incoming energy and move faster as a result; their greater kinetic energies are what is perceived as an increase in the water temperature. Removing heat from the pint of water has the opposite effect: now the molecules lose energy, move more slowly, and the water temperature drops correspondingly.

Temperature is a measure of average molecular kinetic energy

3 Suppose that two liquids, water and ether, are placed in open dishes. Molecules in each are moving in all directions, with a variety of speeds. At any instant some molecules are moving fast enough upward to escape into the air in spite of the attractions of their slower neighbors. By this loss of its faster molecules each liquid gradually evaporates; since the molecules remaining behind are the slower ones, evaporation leaves cool liquids behind. The ether evaporates more quickly (or is more *volatile*) and cools itself more noticeably because the attraction of its particles for one another is smaller and a greater number can escape (Fig. 2.9).

How evaporation occurs

4 When we add heat to a liquid, eventually a temperature is reached at which even molecules of average speed are able to overcome the forces holding them together. Now bubbles of vapor form throughout the liquid, and it begins to boil. This temperature is accordingly called the *boiling point* of the liquid; as we would expect, the boiling point of ether is lower than that of water.

Boiling point

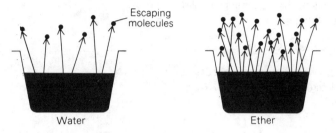

Fig. 2.9 Evaporation. Ether evaporates more rapidly than water because the attractive forces between its molecules are smaller. In each case, the faster molecules escape, and hence the average energy of the remaining molecules is lower and the liquid temperature drops.

Heat of vaporization

5 Whether evaporation takes place spontaneously from an open dish or is aided by heating, the formation of vapor from a liquid requires energy. In the one case energy is supplied from the internal energy of the liquid itself (since the liquid grows cooler), in the other case from the external source of heat. For water at its boiling point, 540 kcal (the *heat of vaporization*) is needed to change each kilogram of liquid into vapor (Fig. 2.10). Here there is no difference in temperature between liquid and vapor, hence no difference in their average molecular kinetic energies. If not into kinetic energy, into what form of molecular energy does the 540 kcal of heat go?

6 Intermolecular forces suggest an answer. In the liquid these forces are strong, because the molecules are close together. To tear the molecules apart, to separate them by the wide distances that exist in the vapor, requires that these strong forces be overcome. Just as a stone thrown upward against the earth's attraction acquires potential energy, so molecules moved apart acquire potential energy. When a vapor condenses into a liquid, its molecules "fall" toward one another under the influence of their mutual attractions, and their potential energy is taken up as heat by the surroundings.

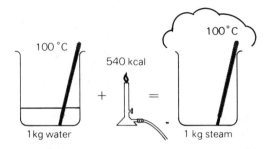

Fig. 2.10 The energy needed to turn a liquid into a gas goes into separating the molecules against the forces that hold them together.

7   The melting of a crystalline solid into a liquid can be understood in a similar way. The particles of a solid are arranged in a definite pattern with strong forces between neighboring ones. To overcome these forces and give the particles the disorderly arrangement of a liquid structure requires that they gain potential energy, just as liquid particles must gain potential energy during evaporation (Fig. 2.11). This potential energy is the *heat of fusion* (80 kcal/kg for water), which must be supplied to melt any crystalline solid and which is given out when the liquid crystallizes again.

Heat of fusion

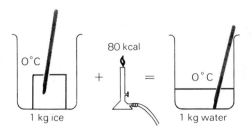

Fig. 2.11 The energy needed to turn a crystalline solid into a liquid goes into converting the orderly arrangement of the particles of the solid into the random arrangement of them in the liquid.

G. Check your understanding

1. Look at the first paragraph and find the words that mean:

- without any pattern or order
- makes up
- of *or* in the inside

2. Using the information given in paragraphs 2 and 3, explain orally what happens when:

- A saucepan of water is heated on a cooker.
- The saucepan of water is taken off the cooker.
- Water evaporates.

3. Now look at the rest of the text and say whether these statements are correct or incorrect:

● Water boils at a higher temperature than ether.	☐
● Evaporation can only take place if a liquid is heated.	☐
● Liquid and vapour never have the same temperature.	☐
● Molecules are further apart in liquid than in vapour.	☐
● The particles of a solid are arranged in a random way.	☐
● Ice is an example of a crystalline solid.	☐

H. Understanding discourse

1. Listen to this conversation between a second year student, James, and a new student, Peter. James is explaining to Peter the layout of the university.

Using the information James gives, label the diagram below. James and Peter are standing at the main entrance.

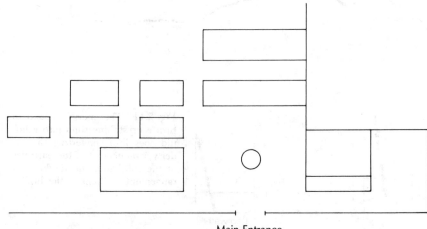

Main Entrance

2. Listen to these instructions given by a lecturer. You can make notes if you want. Then report what the lecturer said, like this:

He said he would be in his office at nine o'clock.

UNIT 4

MINERALS

A. Understanding a printed text (1)

The following text will introduce you to the topic of **minerals**. Look at the way it is divided into sections and paragraphs. Pay attention to the headings and notes in the margin, and to the table.

Now look at these questions:

1. From the headings to the two main sections of the text, what do you expect the two sections will be about?

2. What does the table show?

Read the passage through and find the answers to the questions. Remember, you do not have to understand every word to answer them.

MINERALS

Rocks are composed of homogeneous solids called minerals

1 Rocks are aggregates of substances called *minerals*, which as a rule are crystalline solids with fairly definite compositions and structures. Some rocks, for instance limestone, consist of a single mineral only, but the majority consist of several minerals in varying proportions. The different minerals in a coarse-grained rock like granite are apparent to the eye; in fine-grained rock, the separate minerals can be discerned with the help of a microscope.

What Minerals Are

Chemical reasons for the existence of various kinds of mineral

2 It is not difficult to understand why certain substances occur as minerals and why others do not. We expect to find the more chemically inactive elements, such as gold, platinum, and sulfur, in the free state, whereas chemically active elements, such as sodium, calcium, and chlorine, are always found in combination as compounds. Compounds readily soluble in water, such as sodium chloride, sodium carbonate, and potassium nitrate, form deposits in desert regions but are rare elsewhere. Substances that tend to react with oxygen occur only well below the surface away from the oxygen of the atmosphere. Unstable compounds like phosphorus pentoxide are necessarily absent from the earth's crust.

Silicates are the most abundant minerals

3 Silicates are by far the most abundant minerals; mica, feldspar, and topaz are familiar examples. Carbonates are another important class, its most conspicuous representative being the carbonate of calcium called calcite. Oxides and hydrated oxides include such common materials as hematite (ferric oxide), the chief ore of iron, and bauxite (hydrated aluminum oxide), the chief ore of aluminum. Various metals are obtained from deposits of sulfide minerals, such as galena (lead sulfide) and sphalerite (zinc sulfide). Elements that occur free, or *native*, were mentioned above. Less frequent as minerals are sulfates, phosphates, and chlorides.

4   Unfortunately the study of minerals requires the learning of a special list of names, some of them apparently duplicates of other names. As an example, the mineral whose formula is $CaCO_3$ is given the name *calcite* instead of the chemical name *calcium carbonate*. For this seeming redundancy there are two reasons:

1   The formula $CaCO_3$ describes not only the composition of calcite but also that of aragonite, a less common mineral with a different crystal form, hardness, density, and so on; the chemical name calcium carbonate alone does not distinguish between calcite and aragonite.

2   Calcite often contains small quantities of $MgCO_3$ and $FeCO_3$, and its composition is not precisely represented by the formula $CaCO_3$ because the iron and magnesium carbonates form an integral part of the calcite structure with Fe and Mg atoms replacing some of the Ca atoms in the crystal lattice.

5   Many other mineral formulas besides that of calcite apply to two or more distinct substances, and most minerals show a similar slight variability in composition. Hence chemical names are seldom really applicable, and the student of minerals finds necessary a new nomenclature.

6   Luckily, for present purposes we need only a few additions to our vocabulary. More than 2,000 different minerals are known, but most of these are rare. Even among the commoner minerals, the greater number occur abundantly only in occasional veins, pockets, and layers. The number of minerals that are important constituents of ordinary rocks is surprisingly small, so small that acquaintance with less than a dozen is adequate for an introduction to geology.

Mineral Properties

7   Common minerals are not only limited in number but are also easily recognizable with some experience, often by appearance alone. To distinguish the rarer minerals microscopic examination and chemical tests may be necessary, but for the minerals that compose ordinary rocks such simple physical properties as density, color, hardness (Table 3.1), and crystal form make identification relatively straightforward.

8   In describing the important rock-forming minerals, two properties need special attention: *crystal form* and *cleavage*. Most minerals are crystalline solids, which means that their tiny particles (atoms, ions, or atom groups) are arranged in lattice structures with definite geometric patterns. When a mineral grain develops in a position where its growth is not hindered by neighboring crystals, as in an open cavity, its inner structure expresses itself by the formation of perfect crystals, with smooth faces meeting each other at sharp angles. Every mineral has crystals of a distinctive shape so that well-formed crystals make recognition of a mineral easy; unfortunately good crystals are rare, since mineral grains usually interfere with one another's growth.

Every mineral has a characteristic crystal form

TABLE 3.1

The hardness scale. Each mineral can scratch those lower on the scale and in turn can be scratched by those higher on the scale. A fingernail is about 2.5 in hardness and a knife blade is about 5.5.

1. Talc (softest)
2. Gypsum
3. Calcite
4. Fluorite
5. Apatite
6. Orthoclase
7. Quartz
8. Topaz
9. Corundum
10. Diamond (hardest)

9   Even when well-developed crystals are not present, however, the characteristic lattice structure of a mineral may reveal itself in the property called *cleavage*. This is the tendency of a substance to split along certain planes, which are determined by the arrangement of particles in its lattice. When a mineral grain is struck with a hammer, its cleavage planes are revealed as the preferred directions of breaking; even without actual breaking, the existence of cleavage in a mineral is usually shown by flat, parallel faces and minute parallel cracks. The flat surfaces of mica flakes, for instance, and the ability of mica to peel off in thin sheets show that this mineral has almost perfect cleavage. Some minerals (for example, quartz) have practically no cleavage; when struck they shatter, like glass, along random curved surfaces. The ability to recognize different kinds and degrees of cleavage is an important aid in distinguishing minerals.

B. Check your understanding

Now read the text again carefully, looking up anything you do not understand. Then answer the following questions.

1. What is a *mineral*?

2. What rock is made up of one mineral only?

3. Is chlorine a chemically inactive element?

4. What do sodium chloride, sodium carbonate and potassium have in common?

5. What are the commonest minerals?

6. Why do you need to learn a special list of names to study minerals?

7. How many minerals are known to exist?

8. To start studying geology, how many minerals do you need to know about?

9. What are *crystal form* and *cleavage*?

10. Does every mineral contain crystals of the same shape?

C. Increase your vocabulary

1. Look at the first two paragraphs and say which words are used to mean:

- different materials brought together into a mass
- most/the greater part or number
- distinguish
- can be dissolved in a liquid
- likely to move or change

2. Now look at paragraph 3 and find three words that have the opposite meaning to *rare*.

3. Now look at paragraphs 4, 5 and 6 and say which words in the text you could replace with:

- amounts
- exactly
- rarely
- changeability
- sufficient/enough

4. Now look at paragraph 7 and say which words in the paragraph mean:

- the way something looks
- make up
- uncomplicated/easy

5. Now look at the rest of the passage and explain what these words mean:

- crystalline solid
- grain
- cavity
- plane
- parallel
- flake

6. Complete the following paragraph, using each of these words once: substance, variety, various, abundant, combine, structure, free, compound.

Next to oxygen, the most _____ element in the earth's crust is silicon. Silicon never occurs _____ in nature, but its _____ make up about 87 percent of the rocks and soil under our feet. Nearly all the earth's silicon is either _____ with oxygen alone or with oxygen and one or more metals in the _____ silicate minerals. As a class, these _____ are crystalline solids with high melting points. Their differences in composition and _____ are reflected in a _____ of colours, hardnesses and crystal forms.

D. Check your grammar

ADJECTIVES AND ADVERBS

> **Do you remember?**
> The number of minerals that are *important* constituents of *ordinary* rocks is *surprisingly* small.

1. Complete the following paragraph using the words in brackets:

Clay is an (especial) _____ (interesting) _____ material because of its ability to absorb (large) _____ amounts of water. This ability can be traced to the layered structures of the clay minerals. In many of these minerals, each layer is (electrical) _____ polarised, with one side exhibiting a (slight) _____ (positive) _____ charge and the other a (slight) _____ (negative) _____ charge. (Adjacent) _____ layers are held together by the attractions of the (opposite) _____ charges that face each other; since the layers are only (weak) _____ polarised, the bonds between the layers are (feeble) _____, and (dry) _____ clay crumbles (easy) _____.

Do you remember?
Instead of saying that, he *should have said* . . .

2. Now look at the following notes that a student has made on the text. Say if the notes are accurate or not. If they are not, give the correct version.

- Chemically inactive elements are usually found in compounds. ☐
- Sodium Chloride cannot be easily dissolved in water. ☐
- Potassium nitrate does not occur in deserts. ☐
- Feldspar is not a common mineral. ☐
- Bauxite is the chief ore of iron. ☐
- The Sulphates are a common group of minerals. ☐
- There are 2000 important constituents of ordinary rocks. ☐
- You never need chemical tests to distinguish minerals. ☐
- Crystalline solids show no particular pattern. ☐
- The crystals in minerals all have the same shape. ☐
- Cleavage means the same as "lattice structure". ☐
- Mica shows very poor cleavage. ☐
- Quartz shows a lot of cleavage. ☐

E. Understanding a lecture

Listen to the lecture on six common minerals. The minerals the lecturer will be talking about are quartz, feldspar, mica ferromagnesian minerals, clay minerals and calcite. The lecture is divided into six sections, one on each mineral. Using the information the lecturer gives you, complete as much of the table below as you can. Look at the table first, so you can see what information you are looking for.

Mineral	Formula	Colour	Hardness	Uses

F. Understanding a printed text (2)

Read the following text carefully, looking up anything you do not understand.

ROCKS

1 There is hardly any limit to the variety of rocks on the earth's surface. We find coarse-grained rocks and fine-grained rocks, light rocks and heavy rocks, soft rocks and hard rocks, rocks of all sizes, shapes, and colors. But close study reveals that there is order in this diversity, and a straightforward scheme for classifying rocks has been developed which simplifies the problem of understanding their origins and properties.

Rock Classification

2 At first glance, it is not obvious how rocks can be separated into definite categories. We might decide that a light-colored, coarse-grained rock like granite should belong in a different class from a dark, fine-grained volcanic rock like basalt, but we can find a whole series of rocks with properties transitional between the two, and so we cannot say just where one class ends and the other begins. The basic problem is to make distinctions that are not always clear-cut in nature.

3 Since rocks are composed of minerals, we might guess first that they could be classified on the basis of the kinds and amounts of minerals they contain. But we find that rocks of widely different structures and origins have nearly the same mineral composition, and so we would be grouping together rocks of obviously different types. A classification based on chemical composition encounters the same difficulty, since it places in the same pigeonhole rocks that have little else in common; it has the further disadvantage that chemical compositions are not evident in the field but require laboratory analysis. We might disregard composition and classify rocks according to their origin. This would be an excellent method if it could be applied to all rocks, but the sad fact is that we simply do not know how some rocks were formed and the origin of many others can be determined only after lengthy study.

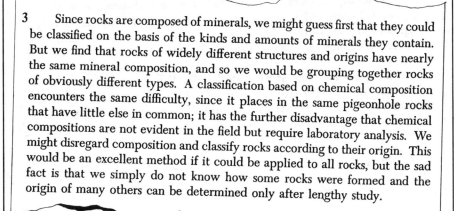

Problems of rock classification

4   Evidently we expect a classification of rocks to fulfill several different purposes. We should like it to summarize something about the origins of different rocks, about their compositions, and about their structures, and at the same time we should like to be able to apply it to rocks as we find them in the field. These objectives cannot all be satisfied at the same time. Our recourse is to adopt a compromise, a classification that will accomplish each purpose as well as possible without slighting the others. The particular compromise we shall use is not the only possible one, but it is justified by its simplicity and convenience.

5   A fundamental division of rocks into three main groups according to origin is agreed on by nearly all geologists:

The three main types of rock are igneous, sedimentary, and metamorphic

1   *Igneous rocks* are those that have cooled from a molten state. Some of these can be observed in process of formation, for instance when molten lava cools on the side of a volcano. For others an igneous origin is inferred from their composition and structure. Two-thirds of crustal rocks are igneous, and the bedrock under the oceans and continents falls into this category.

2   *Sedimentary rocks* consist of materials derived from other rocks and deposited by water, wind, or glacial ice. Some consist of separate rock fragments cemented together; others contain material precipitated from solution in water. Although sedimentary rocks make up only about 8 percent of the crust, three-quarters of surface rocks are of this kind.

Although most of the crust consists of igneous rocks, the majority of surface rocks are sedimentary

3   *Metamorphic rocks* are rocks that have been changed, or metamorphosed, by heat and pressure deep under the earth's surface. The changes produced may involve the formation of new minerals or simply the recrystallization of minerals already present.

In the following sections we shall describe the important rock types in each major group. Emphasis here will be on the characteristics by which different rocks can be recognized; in future chapters we shall deal at greater length with processes of rock formation.

Igneous Rocks

6   The structure of igneous rocks is characterized by random arrangement of grains, by ragged crystal borders, by intertwinings and embayments such as one might expect in a mass of crystals growing together and interfering with one another's development. In coarse-grained rocks like granite, this structure is visible to the naked eye; in fine-grained rocks it is revealed by the microscope. The principal constituents of these rocks are always minerals containing silicon: quartz, feldspar, mica, and the ferromagnesian group.

7   The siliceous liquids from which igneous rocks form are thick, viscous materials resembling melted glass both in properties and in composition. Sometimes, in fact, molten lava has the right composition and cools rapidly enough to form a natural glass—the black, shiny rock called *obsidian*. Usually, however, cooling is slow enough to allow crystalline minerals to form. If cooling is fairly rapid and if the molten material is highly viscous, the resulting rock may consist of minute crystals or partly of crystals and partly of glass. If cooling is extremely slow, mineral grains have an opportunity to grow large and a coarse-grained rock is formed. The grain size of an igneous rock, therefore, reveals something about its history and gives us one logical basis for classification.

8   Mineral composition provides a convenient means of further classification. Nearly all igneous rocks contain feldspar and one or more of the ferromagnesian minerals; many contain quartz as well. A division of igneous rocks based on relative amounts of these three mineral types is shown in Table 3.2. Thus a coarse-grained rock containing quartz, feldspar, and black mica is granite; a fine-grained rock with no quartz and with feldspar in excess of the dark constituents is andesite, and so on. Not all igneous rocks by any means are shown in the table, but these six are the most important.

9   This classification is convenient for several reasons:

1   Grain size and usually mineral composition can be determined from inspection in the field. Except for a few fine-grained types, an igneous rock can be named without detailed laboratory study.

TABLE 3.2

Some igneous rocks. These have solidified from a molten state.

Mineral composition	Coarse-grained rocks (intrusive)	Fine-grained rocks (extrusive)
Quartz Feldspar Ferromagnesian minerals	Granite	Rhyolite
No quartz Feldspar predominant Ferromagnesian minerals	Diorite	Andesite
No quartz Feldspar Ferromagnesian minerals predominant	Gabbro	Basalt

Igneous rocks have solidified from an originally molten state

Obsidian is a glassy rock of volcanic origin

2 Even if a rock is too fine for its mineral content to be easily determined, its color often shows its place in the table. Granite and rhyolite, which contain only a little ferromagnesian material, are nearly always light-colored; gabbro and basalt, with abundant ferromagnesian minerals, are characteristically dark; diorite and andesite usually have intermediate shades. Granite and rhyolite are sometimes designated as *felsic* rocks (because of their large feldspar content) and gabbro and basalt as *mafic* rocks (because of their ferromagnesian content).

3 Grain size usually gives an indication not only of the rate of cooling but also of the environment in which a rock was cooled. Sufficiently rapid cooling to give fine-grained rocks occurs most commonly when molten lava reaches the earth's surface from a volcano and spreads out in a thin flow exposed to the atmosphere. Since fine grain size usually betrays volcanic origin, rhyolite, andesite, and basalt are often called *volcanic* or *extrusive* rocks.

Coarse-grained rocks, on the other hand, have cooled sufficiently slowly for large crystals to have formed, which must have occurred well beneath the earth's surface. Such rocks are now exposed to view only because erosion has carried away the material that once covered them. Since these rocks do not reach the surface as liquids but are intruded into spaces occupied by other rocks, they are often called *intrusive* rocks.

4 The change in mineral composition from top to bottom in Table 3.2 roughly parallels a steady change in chemical composition. Granite and rhyolite are relatively rich in silicon and aluminum; gabbro and basalt contain abundant iron and magnesium.

Sedimentary Rocks

10 Sediments laid down by water, wind, or ice are consolidated into rock by the weight of overlying deposits and by the gradual cementing of their grains with material deposited from underground water. The resulting rocks are usually characterized by the presence of distinct, somewhat rounded grains that have not grown together like the crystals of igneous rocks. A few sedimentary rocks, however, consist of intergrown mineral grains formed by precipitation from solution in water. Since sediments are normally deposited in layers, the majority of sedimentary rocks have a banded appearance owing to slight differences in color or grain size from one layer to the next. Sedimentary rocks may often be recognized at a glance by the presence of fossils—remains of plants or animals interred with the sediments as they were laid down.

G. Check your understanding

1. Look at the first paragraph and say which words have the same meaning as:

- scarcely
- makes easy
- shows

2. Look at the first paragraph in the section 'Rock Classification'. The writer states a basic problem. What is it?

3. In paragraph 3 the writer considers two possible answers to the problem. What are these possible answers?

4. In the same paragraph, the writer rejects these possible answers. Why does he reject them?

5. In paragraph 4, the writer says what he expects from a rock classification system. What are his expectations?

6. What basis does the writer accept for the classification of rocks?

7. Explain in your own words the difference between igneous, sedimentary and metamorphic rocks?

8. Now look at these notes. What does each note refer to?

Example
   rocks deposited by water, wind or glacial ice — refers to sedimentary rocks

- a black shiny rock formed by molten lava
- mainly composed of minerals containing silicon
- shows us something about the origin of a rock, and therefore gives us one basis for classification
- another means of classification
- for example, granite and rhyolite
- for example, gabbro and basalt

9. Now look at these terms and decide what note you would make for yourself on:

- volcanic/extrusive rocks
- rock colour

10. Using your own words, write a summary of the rock classification system described in the first section (paragraphs 2–5) of the text.

H. Understanding discourse

A lecturer is talking about some metamorphic rocks. Metamorphic rocks are formed from sedimentary and igneous rocks under the influence of heat and pressure. One of the students listening to the lecturer has put the information in a table. But he has got some of the information wrong. Listen to the lecturer and correct the student's table.

SOME METAMORPHIC ROCKS

Group	Type	Constituents	Origin
Foliated rocks	Slate	Mica, and always quartz, both in microscopic grains	Shale
	Schist	Mica and/or a ferromagnesian mineral, usually quartz also	Shale or coarse-grained rocks
Foliated Banded	Quartz	Gneiss, feldspar, mica	Various
	Marble	Chiefly calcite	Sandstone
	Quartzite	Chiefly quartz	Limestone

THE ATMOSPHERE

A. Understanding a printed text (1)

The following text will introduce you to the topic of the **atmosphere**. Look at the way it is divided into sections and paragraphs. Pay attention to the headings and notes in the margins, and to the illustrations and captions.

Now look at these questions:

1. What is explained in the first section?

2. What two main processes are described in the second section?

Read the passage through and find the answers to the questions. Remember, you do not have to understand every word to answer them.

Properties of the atmosphere

Composition

1   The principal constituents of the atmosphere and their average abundances are given in Fig. 4.1. Water vapor is also present but to a variable extent, ranging from nearly none to about 4 percent. The lower atmosphere also contains a considerable quantity of small, solid particles of different kinds, such as soot, bits of rock and soil, salt grains from the evaporation of seawater droplets, and spores, pollen, and bacteria.

2   The blue color of the sky is due to the scattering of sunlight by gas molecules and dust particles in the atmosphere (Fig. 4.2). Blue light is scattered most; hence skylight, which consists of scattered sunlight, is predominantly blue, and the sun itself appears a little more yellowish or reddish than it would if there were no atmosphere. At sunrise and sunset, when the sun's light has a long path through the atmosphere, the scattering is greatest, and the sun may be a brilliant red. Above the atmosphere the sky appears black, and the moon, stars, and planets are visible to astronauts in the daytime.

Oxygen–Carbon Dioxide Cycle

3   Nitrogen and oxygen are important biologically, and each has a characteristic cycle of interaction with living things. Nitrogen is a key ingredient of the amino acids of which all proteins consist, and certain bacteria are able to convert atmospheric nitrogen into nitrogen compounds which plants can utilize in manufacturing amino acids.

4   Plants also combine carbon dioxide from the air with water absorbed through their roots to form carbohydrates in the process of *photosynthesis,* with oxygen as a by-product. Animals obtain the carbohydrates and amino acids they need by eating plants (or other animals that eat plants). Plants and animals both derive energy by using atmospheric oxygen to convert carbon in their foods to carbon dioxide. Thus the oxygen–carbon dioxide cycle is an essential aspect of all plant and animal life (Fig. 4.3).

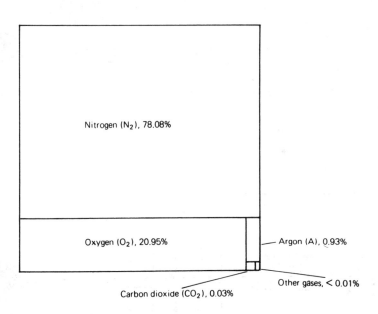

Nitrogen (N_2), 78.08%

Oxygen (O_2), 20.95%

Argon (A), 0.93%

Other gases, < 0.01%

Carbon dioxide (CO_2), 0.03%

Fig. 4.1 Composition of dry air near ground level. The figures given are percentages by volume. Water vapor is also present in the atmosphere at concentrations that vary from nearly 0 to as much as 4 percent.

5 The carbohydrates formed by photosynthesis are complex compounds of carbon, hydrogen, and oxygen, and include sugar, starch, and cellulose—the first two familiar as important nutrients, the last the chief constituent of cell walls in plants (wood is mostly cellulose). Photosynthesis can be represented by the equation

$$CO_2 + H_2O + \text{sunlight} \longrightarrow \text{carbohydrates} + O_2$$

The energy in sunlight is not taken up directly by the carbon dioxide and water but instead by the substance *chlorophyll*, which is part of the green coloring matter of leaves; the chlorophyll is not permanently changed but serves to pass on the energy it absorbs to the reacting molecules in a complicated way. About 70 billion tons of carbon dioxide are cycled through plants each year.

6 The reverse reaction, called *respiration*, is the process by which living things obtain the energy they require for growth, motion, and so forth. Like photosynthesis, respiration occurs in a series of complex steps, but its overall result is straightforward:

$$\text{Carbohydrates} + O_2 \longrightarrow CO_2 + H_2O + \text{energy}$$

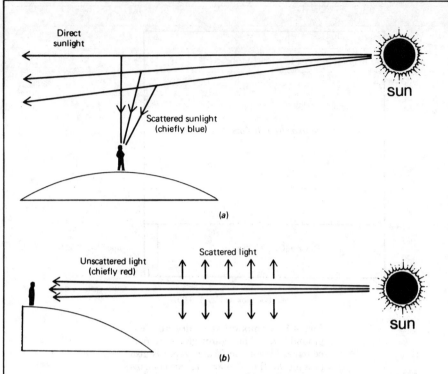

Fig. 4.2 (*a*) The preferential scattering of blue light in the atmosphere is responsible for the blue color of the sky. (*b*) The remaining direct sunlight is reddish, which is the reason for the red color of the sun at sunrise and sunset.

7   Photosynthesis not only maintains the oxygen content of the atmosphere but was apparently responsible for it in the first place. The early atmosphere of the earth, which is thought to have consisted of gases emitted during volcanic action, contained oxygen only in combination with other elements in such compounds as water (H_2O), carbon dioxide (CO_2), and sulfur dioxide (SO_2). Primitive organisms, which probably obtained their own energy by fermentation, eventually began to produce free oxygen by photosynthesis, and in time the oxygen content of the atmosphere increased to the point where more complex organisms could evolve. In addition to the oxygen now present in the atmosphere, photosynthesis is believed to account for the much larger quantity combined with other elements in the oxides, carbonates, and sulfates found in sediments and sedimentary rocks.

B. Check your understanding

Now read the text again carefully, looking up anything you do not understand. Then answer the following questions.

1. Fig. 4.1 shows the composition of dry air at ground level. What else is present in the atmosphere that is not shown in Fig. 4.1?

2. What is the purpose of Fig. 4.2?

3. How does an animal like a lion obtain carbohydrates?

4. What is photosynthesis?

5. What is the reverse process to photosynthesis?

6. How is the word chlorophyll explained in the text?

7. How did oxygen occur in the early atmosphere?

8. Oxygen is now found in the atmosphere. Where else is it found?

C. Increase your vocabulary

1. Look at the first section and say which word or words in the text have the same meaning as:

- mainly
- for this reason
- is caused by
- very bright

2. What words in the first section are used for:

- a fine powder formed by flowers, and carried from flower to flower by the wind or by insects
- germs or single cells by which a flowerless plant reproduces itself

3. Now look at paragraphs 3, 4, 5 in the second section, and say what words in these paragraphs you could replace with:

- essential
- get from, obtain
- change

4. Using your dictionary, look at the rest of the second section and explain the words below:

- emit
- fermentation
- organism
- primitive
- reverse
- account for

5. Using the information in the text, can you complete the following figure that illustrates the oxygen–carbon dioxide cycle?

1. _____

2. _____

3. _____

4. _____

5. _____

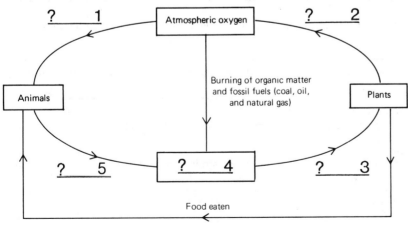

Fig. 4.3 The oxygen–carbon dioxide cycle.

D. Check your grammar

1. Look at this timetable for the Earth Sciences department at a university. The time now is 6 o'clock on the Wednesday evening. Say what has already happened and what has not happened yet.

	MONDAY	TUESDAY	WEDNESDAY	THURSDAY	FRIDAY
09.00	Prof. Jones (L) Energy	Prof. Jones (S) Energy	Mr Roberts (L) Properties of the earth	Mr Roberts (L) The moving earth	Mr Roberts (S) The earth in space
10.00	Mr Smith (L) Earth materials	Prof. Jones (T) Energy	Mr Roberts (L) The earth in space	Prof. Jones (S) Matter	Mr Smith (T) Soil
11.00	Mr Smith (L) Minerals	Mr Smith (L) Rocks	Mr Smith (L) Soil	Mr Roberts (S) The earth as a planet	Prof. Jones (T) Matter
14.00			Mr Smith (S) Earth materials	Mr Smith (T) Minerals	Mr Smith (T) Rocks

L = lecture; S = seminar; T = tutorial

2. Now complete the conversation between two students below. Be careful which tense you use!

Alan: I (not see) _____ you at Professor Jones' lecture yesterday, John. Where (be) _____ you?

John: I (forget) _____ all about it. I (start) _____ the essay two days ago and I (want) _____ to finish it before the lecture. It's a pity. It's the first lecture I (miss) _____ so far this term.

Alan: I (not complete) _____ the reading for that essay yet. I (go) _____ to the library yesterday, but the books (not be) _____ there.

John: I (never find) _____ the books I need in the library since I (come) _____ to this university a year ago. Someone (just take) _____ them out each time I go there. Something ought to be done about . . . .

E. Understanding a lecture

Listen to the lecture on regions of the atmosphere. Using the information the lecturer gives you, answer the questions below. Also label the diagram. The lecture is divided into sections. Listen to each section twice.

Section 1

Are these statements correct or incorrect?

• The subject of last week's lecture was the properties of the atmosphere.	☐
• The lecturer expects all the students to have climbed mountains.	☐
• If you climb a mountain, the air gets colder but not thinner.	☐
• In the lower atmosphere, the temperature falls at 6.5°C/km of altitude.	☐
• The temperature falls at 3.6°F per mile.	☐

Section 2

Are these statements correct or incorrect?

• At higher altitudes the temperature continues to drop.	☐
• Instruments to measure temperature are only carried in aeroplanes.	☐
• At even higher altitudes, the pressure continues to drop.	☐
• At even higher altitudes, the temperature continues to drop in the same way as at lower altitudes.	☐

Label the diagram in the way the lecturer tells you to.

F. Understanding a printed text (2)

Read the following text carefully, looking up anything you do not understand.

The Ozone Layer

1   Many scientists prefer to regard the stratosphere and mesosphere as being different parts of the same layer, because apart from temperature their properties are similar. Sounding balloons filled with hydrogen or helium routinely penetrate the stratosphere with instruments of various kinds and send down data by radio to ground stations; some aircraft, too, are capable of exploring the stratosphere. The still higher elevations of the mesosphere require rocket-borne apparatus if direct measurements are to be made, but a number of experimental methods have been devised that enable observatories on the ground to determine some of the physical properties of this part of the atmosphere.

2   The most striking feature of the stratosphere and the lower mesosphere is the presence of *ozone,* a form of oxygen whose molecules contain three oxygen atoms instead of the usual two. The chemical symbol for ozone is accordingly O_3. Ozone is an excellent absorber of ultraviolet radiation; so excellent, in fact, that the relatively small amount of ozone in the upper atmosphere completely filters out the dangerous short-wavelength ultraviolet radiation emitted by the sun. Living things on earth would certainly have evolved very differently without the protection of the ozone layer, since few of today's organisms could survive exposure to solar ultraviolet rays at their full strength.

Ozone in the upper atmosphere absorbs ultraviolet radiation from the sun

3   The ozone layer lies between 15 and 55 km. At its maximum density less than 1 molecule in 4 million is O_3—hardly an impressive concentration for so efficient a filter. At sea-level temperature and pressure, all the ozone in the atmosphere would form a layer less than an inch thick. The elevated temperatures of the upper stratosphere and lower mesosphere are due to the heating effect of the solar ultraviolet energy absorbed at the top of the ozone layer.

4   Why is the ozone content of the atmosphere concentrated in a particular region instead of being more or less uniformly distributed? The first step in the formation of an ozone molecule is the breaking up of an O_2 molecule into two O atoms by solar ultraviolet light. The second step is the attachment of an O atom to an O_2 molecule to form O_3. The rate of ozone production thus depends upon both the O_2 concentration and the intensity of solar ultraviolet light. At extremely high altitudes there are not enough O_2 molecules for an appreciable amount of O_3 to be formed. Between 15 and 55 km above the ground, however, the atmosphere is dense enough for the production of O_3 but not so dense that the unstable ozone molecules break up into $O_2 + O$ too often in collisions with other molecules. At lower altitudes the ultraviolet light has already been absorbed so no ozone can come into being there except as a result of lightning strokes in the lower atmosphere.

Origin of the ozone layer

The Ionosphere

5   In the year 1901 Marconi was able to send radio signals across the Atlantic Ocean for the first time. Radio waves, like light waves, tend to travel in straight lines, and the curvature of the earth therefore apparently presents an insuperable obstacle to long-distance radio communication. For this reason Marconi's achievement came as a great surprise. In a short time, however, Oliver Heaviside in England and Arthur Kennelly in the United States suggested that the effect could be caused by a reflecting layer high up in the atmosphere. Such a layer, together with the sea, could channel radio waves from one side of the Atlantic to the other (Fig. 4.7). Electromagnetic theory was able to predict the mechanism of the reflection: If some of the atoms and molecules in the upper atmosphere are ionized (become electrically charged) by the action of solar ultraviolet light and x-rays, the resulting assembly of charged particles will behave precisely like a mirror to radio waves (though not to the shorter-wavelength light waves).

6   Experimental confirmation of the presence of ionized layers high up in the atmosphere followed, and today the region properly called the thermosphere is often referred to as the *ionosphere*. During the day the ionosphere has four distinct layers, D, E, F_1, and F_2 in order of ascending altitude. At night the D layer disappears, the E layer weakens, and the F_1 and F_2 layers coalesce into a single weak F layer. The D layer tends to absorb rather than reflect radio waves, which is why radio reception from distant stations is best at night when this layer is absent. Solar outbursts (see Chap. 13) from time to time increase the ionization in the D layer and produce radio blackouts that prevent long-range radio communication.

Ionospheric layers reflect radio waves and so permit long-distance communication

Structure of the ionosphere

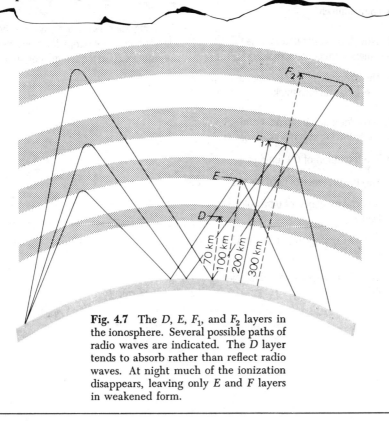

Fig. 4.7 The D, E, F_1, and F_2 layers in the ionosphere. Several possible paths of radio waves are indicated. The D layer tends to absorb rather than reflect radio waves. At night much of the ionization disappears, leaving only E and F layers in weakened form.

G. Check your understanding

1. Look at the first paragraph and say which of the following statements is correct:

- The stratosphere and mesosphere

  are exactly the same ☐

  differ in their temperatures ☐

  have the same temperature ☐

  have different properties except for
  temperature ☐

- Information about the stratosphere is usually gathered

  only by rockets ☐

  only by ground stations ☐

  by balloons ☐

  only by special aeroplanes ☐

2. Now look at paragraph 2 and say which words have the same meaning as:

- very good
- attracting interest/attention
- comparatively

3. Now look at paragraph 3. Is this statement correct or incorrect?

- The ozone layer in the upper atmosphere is less than an inch thick. ☐

4. Now look at paragraph 4 and say which of the following statements is correct:

- The formation of O_3 requires

  only the presence of O_2 molecules ☐

  only the existence of ultraviolet light ☐

  neither O_2 molecules nor ultraviolet light ☐

  both O_2 molecules and ultraviolet light ☐

- At a height of 15 to 55 km above the earth, O_3 molecules

  do not exist ☐

  always break up ☐

  sometimes break up ☐

  never break up ☐

5. Now look at paragraph 5 and say which words have the same or almost the same meaning as:

- roundness
- foresee
- gathering/meeting together
- hindrance
- are inclined to

6. Now look at paragraph 6 and say which words have the opposite meaning to:

- strengthens
- denial
- separate
- descending
- nearby

7. Using your own words, write a short description of the ozone layer and the ionosphere. Use the information in the text.

H. Understanding discourse

Listen to this lecturer explaining what you must do if there is a fire in the building. You are in room 401. If there was a fire now, where would you go?

_____

_____

_____

_____

_____

_____

_____

_____

The following short test is for you to check whether you are learning the skills you will need to study Earth Sciences in English. It is for *your* information. It is *not* an examination. You may use a dictionary.

A. Reading

Read the following text and then answer the questions.

MOISTURE

The evaporation of seawater is responsible for most of the water vapor in the atmosphere, with the rest coming from the evaporation of water from lakes, rivers, moist soil, and vegetation. More water falls as rain and snow on landmasses than is lost by them through evaporation, which compensates for the runoff of continental water to the oceans by rivers and streams. In turn, the oceans lose more water by evaporation than they gain by precipitation (Fig. 4.8). On the average, 9 or 10 days elapse between the evaporation of a certain sample of water and its precipitation as rain or snow. Relatively little of the earth's surface water is in the form of atmospheric moisture; if all the water vapor in the atmosphere were condensed, it would form a layer only about an inch thick.

Relative Humidity

Air is said to be *saturated* with water vapor when it contains the maximum amount that will evaporate at a given temperature. Air is unsaturated when its amount of water vapor is less than this limiting value, since it is capable of holding more water vapor. In effect, air may be regarded as a sort of sponge, filled more or less completely with water vapor. Actually, of course, the air has nothing to do with evaporation; if no air existed, vapor would still escape from bodies of water. But, since air is the agent that transports water vapor from one region to another and since air is the medium in which water vapor condenses as clouds, fog, rain, or snow, we shall find it convenient to think of the air as "taking up" and "holding" different amounts of vapor.

We usually describe air as humid if it is saturated or nearly saturated, as dry if it is far from saturated. Humid weather is oppressive because little moisture can evaporate from the skin into saturated air, and so perspiration does not produce its usual cooling effect. Very dry air is harmful to the skin 26 because its moisture evaporates too rapidly. The moisture content of air is usually specified in terms of *relative humidity*, a number indicating the degree to·which air is saturated with water vapor. A relative humidity of 100 percent means that the air is completely saturated with water vapor; 50 percent means that the air contains half of the maximum vapor it could hold, and 0 percent means perfectly dry air. Since water vapor is continually being added to air by evaporation and periodically removed by condensation into clouds and precipitation as rain and snow, the humidity of the atmosphere is extremely variable from day to day and from one region to another.

The amount of moisture that air can hold increases with temperature. If air saturated at 20°C is heated to 40°C, it can take up more water vapor and so is no longer saturated (in other words, its relative humidity decreases, although the amount of water vapor does not change). If, on the other hand, air saturated at 20°C is cooled to 0°C, some of its water vapor must condense out as liquid water, since at the lower temperature the air can hold only about one-fourth as much vapor as it contained originally. Further, if air at 40°C containing water vapor corresponding to 100 percent relative humidity at 43 20°C is cooled to 0°C, it grows steadily more saturated until a temperature of 20°C is reached, after which it remains saturated down to 0°C as some of its vapor condenses out. Thus any sample of ordinary air on heating grows less saturated and on cooling grows more saturated. If the cooling is continued past the saturation point, some liquid water (or ice) must condense out.

Answer these questions.

1. Most of the water vapour in the atmosphere comes from:

- rivers ☐
- lakes ☐
- the seas
- the land ☐

2. *Moist* is another word for:

- slightly wet ☐
- dry ☐
- very wet ☐
- rainy ☐

3. It takes 9–10 days for moisture to:

- evaporate from the oceans ☐
- evaporate and fall again ☐
- change from rain to snow ☐
- evaporate and condense into layers ☐

4. Air is said to be unsaturated when:

- it contains no water vapour at all ☐
- it cannot contain any more water vapour ☐
- it contains only a little water vapour ☐
- it could hold more water vapour ☐

5. Is this statement correct or incorrect?

- Air is what creates evaporation. ☐

6. In line 26 the word *its* refers to:

- dry air ☐
- evaporation ☐
- skin ☐
- moisture ☐

7. *Relative humidity* is a term which describes

- how much moisture there is in the air ☐
- a particular number ☐
- evaporation ☐
- the speed at which water vapour is created ☐

8. Is this statement correct or incorrect?

- There is only one reason why the humidity of the atmosphere changes a great deal. ☐

9. Is this statement correct or incorrect?

- Saturated air cannot hold more vapour even if it is heated. ☐

10. The word *it* in line 43 refers to:

- air ☐
- water vapour ☐
- relative humidity ☐
- temperature ☐

B. Writing

Read the following text. Then, using your own words, explain the differences between the various kinds of soil described in the text.

Types of Soil

A wide variety of soil types have been identified, most of which fall into the four broad classes of podzolic soils, latosols, chernozems, and desert soils.

1 *Podzolic soils* are mainly found in cool, moist climates under coniferous or partly coniferous forests, as in most of northern Europe and Canada. They are gray in color because most of the iron and other soluble minerals have been washed away ("leached out"), and are acid, which discourages the work of earthworms and other organisms to the extent that there is a sharp line of demarcation between a thin upper layer of partly decayed plant matter and a mineral layer underneath with little organic content. Much of central Europe and the eastern United States is covered with gray-brown, red, and yellow podzolic soils which owe their color and agricultural productivity in part to a smaller degree of acidity, which inhibits leaching and is more favorable for the flourishing of soil organisms.

2 *Latosols* are typical of rain forests in hot, humid climates, and they are prevalent in Brazil, west and central Africa, and southeast Asia. Latosols are rich in iron and aluminum oxides; they are very porous and have been largely leached of plant nutrients required for cultivation. Latosol soils are red or yellow in color.

3 *Chernozem* is a Russian word meaning "black earth," and the chernozemic soils are indeed black or dark brown in color. They are found in temperate, subhumid climates and were formed under vegetation of prairie grasses rather than forests. Southern Russia, a north-south belt in the central United States, and parts of South America, India, Canada, China, and Australia have soils of this kind, which are extremely fertile.

4 *Desert soils* are of various kinds but, being formed in arid regions with little vegetation, are all light in color due to the lack of organic content. There is an abundance of soluble minerals, and sometimes a crust of alkaline and salt materials is present on the surface. The richness in soluble minerals partly compensates for the absence of humus, and many desert soils can be cultivated with proper irrigation.

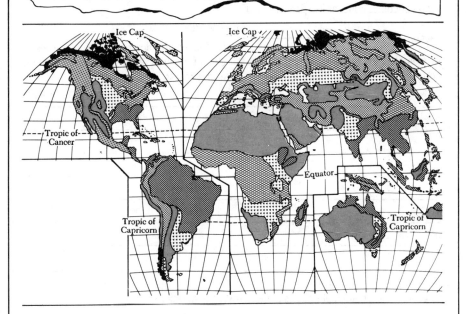

Broad Schematic Soil Map

Tundra Soils—Dwarf shrub- and moss-covered soils of frigid climates.

Podzolic Soils—Forested soils of humid, temperate climates; includes many areas of organic soils.

Chernozemic Soils—Grass-covered soils of subhumid, semiarid temperate climates; includes some soils of wet-dry tropical savannas such as black and dark gray clays.

Desertic (Arid) Soils—Sparsely shrub or grass-covered soils of arid, temperate, and tropical climates; includes large areas of Lithosols and Regosols.

Latosolic Soils—Forested and savanna-covered soils of humid and wet-dry tropical and subtropical climates.

Soils of Mountains—Stony soils (Lithosols) with inclusions of one or more above soils, depending on climate and vegetation, which vary with elevation and latitude.

C. Listening

You will now hear part of a lecture. After you have listened to each section, answer the questions below.

Section 1

1. The first thing the lecturer is going to talk about is:

rain	☐
snow	☐
clouds	☐
condensation	☐

2. Is this statement correct or incorrect?

You can sometimes find condensation on the windows of a house. ☐

3. Is this statement correct or incorrect?

Gas becomes hotter as it expands. ☐

Section 2

4. Complete the following statements correctly.

1.

2.

3.

When a warm, moist air mass moves upwards:

the pressure rises	☐
the pressure remains the same	☐
the pressure drops	☐
the pressure first rises and then drops	☐

The small drops or ice crystals are formed by:

dust particles alone	☐
water vapour alone	☐
salt particles alone	☐
water vapour, salt and dust particles	☐

Section 3

5. The lecturer describes three processes of cloud formation. Write a very short note on each process.

Section 4

6. Look at the photographs opposite and answer the questions :

What cloud types are shown in the pictures? What do they look like?

	Type	Appearance
Picture 1:		
Picture 2:		
Picture 3:		

PICTURE 1

PICTURE 2

PICTURE 3

Section 5

What types of cloud are:
altostratus_____

nimbostratus_____

UNIT 6

THE DYNAMIC ATMOSPHERE

A. Understanding a printed text (1)

The following text continues the theme of Unit 5, the **atmosphere**. Look at the way it is divided into sections and paragraphs. Pay attention to the headings and notes in the margins, and to the illustrations and captions.

Now look at these questions:

1. What is the main task of the atmosphere?
2. What is the difference between *weather* and *climate*?

3. What is insolation?
4. What is meant by the *greenhouse effect*?
5. What does Fig. 4.10 illustrate?

Read the passage through and find the answers to the questions. Remember, you do not have to understand every word to answer them.

THE DYNAMIC ATMOSPHERE

1 The science of meteorology is concerned with what may be thought of as a vast, automatic air-conditioning system. Our spinning planet is heated strongly at the equator, feebly at the poles, and its moisture is concentrated in the great ocean basins. It is the task of the atmosphere, from our point of view, to redistribute this heat and moisture so that large areas of the land surface will be habitable. Air conditioning by the atmosphere is far from perfect; it fails miserably in desert regions, on mountain summits, in far northern and southern latitudes. On sultry nights in midsummer or on bitter January mornings we may question its efficiency even in our favored part of the world. But the atmosphere does succeed in making a surprisingly large amount of the earth's surface fit for human habitation.

2   The two chief functions of any air-conditioning system are the regulation of air temperature and humidity. In addition to these, we expect the atmosphere to perform a third function: it must provide us at intervals with rain or snow. The weather and climate of a given locality describe how effectively these functions are performed. *Weather* refers to the temperature, humidity, pressure, cloudiness, and rainfall at a certain time; *climate* is a summary of weather conditions over a period of years. Important in a description of climate is the variability of temperature and rainfall with the seasons; an outstanding feature of the climate of North Dakota is its extreme warmth in summer and extreme cold in winter, whereas the climate of southern California is characterized by equable year-round temperatures and by a concentration of rainfall in the winter months. Local barometric pressures and the intensity and direction of wind may be important in descriptions of weather and climate.

Atmospheric Energy

3   The energy that warms the air, evaporates water, and drives the winds comes to us from the sun. Solar energy arriving at the upper atmosphere is called *insolation* (for *in*coming *sol*ar radi*ation*) and amounts to 20 kcal/min on each square meter of area perpendicular to the sun's rays. (A kilocalorie, we recall from Chap. 2, is the energy in the form of heat that can raise the temperature of one kilogram of water by one degree Celsius.) In order to understand how energy is provided to the atmosphere by insolation, we must first examine the *greenhouse effect*.

Insolation

4   It is a fundamental observation that every object gives off energy in the form of electromagnetic waves, with the intensity and predominant wavelength depending upon the temperature of the object. The hotter the object, the more energy it emits and the shorter the average wavelength. Thus the sun, whose surface temperature is about 5700°C, is extremely bright and its radiation is principally visible light; the earth, whose surface temperature averages about 15°C, is a feebler source of energy and its radiation is concentrated in the long-wavelength infrared part of the spectrum to which the eye is not sensitive. The interior of a greenhouse is warmer than the outside because sunlight can enter through its windows but the infrared radiation that the warm interior gives off cannot penetrate glass, so the incoming energy is trapped.

The greenhouse effect

5   About 34 percent of insolation is directly reflected back into space, mainly by clouds. The atmosphere absorbs perhaps 19 percent, with ozone, water vapor, and water droplets in clouds taking up most of this amount. Thus 47 percent of the total insolation reaches the earth's surface, where it is absorbed and converted into heat. The warm earth then reradiates its excess energy back into the atmosphere, but the energy now is in the form of long-wavelength infrared radiation. These long waves are readily absorbed by atmospheric carbon dioxide and water vapor. The molecules of these gases, speeded up by absorption of heat energy, give some of this energy to other air molecules during collisions. Thus the chief source of atmospheric heat is radiation from the earth, not the energy of direct sunlight. The atmosphere is, in effect, a giant greenhouse.

Weather phenomena are powered by solar energy reradiated from the earth

6   If the earth had no atmosphere, its heated surface would quickly radiate back into space all the energy that reaches it from the sun. Like the moon, the earth would grow intensely hot during the day, unbearably cold at night. An atmosphere effectively prevents these extremes of temperature; its continual movement makes impossible undue heating of any one region by day, and its ability to absorb and hold the earth's radiation prevents the rapid escape of heat by night. Our atmosphere acts as an efficient trap, admitting the energy of sunlight freely but hindering its escape.

The atmosphere prevents temperature extremes from occurring

7   How hot the atmosphere becomes over any particular region depends on a number of factors. Air near the equator is on the average much warmer than air near the poles, because the sun's vertical rays are more effective in

heating the surface than the slanting rays of polar regions (Fig. 4.9). Air over a mountain summit may become warm at midday but cools quickly because it is thinner and contains less carbon dioxide and water vapor than air at lower elevations. A region covered with clouds usually has lower air temperatures than an adjacent region in sunlight. Because the temperature of water is changed more slowly than that of rocks and soil by absorption or loss of radiation, the atmosphere near large bodies of water is usually cooler by day and warmer by night than the atmosphere over regions far from water. Desert regions commonly show abrupt changes in air temperature between day and night because so little water vapor is present to absorb heat radiation. The atmospheric temperatures of some regions are influenced profoundly by winds and by ocean currents.

8   Because the earth's average temperature does not change by very much with time, there must be a balance between incoming and outgoing energy. That such a balance does indeed occur can be seen with the help of Fig. 4.10, which shows how the rates at which radiant energy enters and leaves the earth vary with latitude.

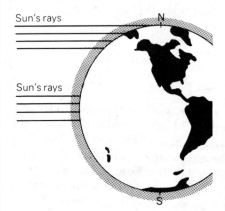

Fig. 4.9 Air near the equator is on the average much warmer than air near the poles because the sun's vertical rays at the equator are more effective in heating the surface than the slanting rays of polar regions.

Winds and ocean currents carry energy from the tropics to the high latitudes

9   More energy arrives at the tropical regions than is lost there, and the opposite is true at the polar regions. Why then do not the tropics grow warmer and warmer while the poles grow colder and colder? The answer is to be found in the motions of air and water that shift energy from the regions of surplus to the regions of deficit. About 80 percent of the energy transport around the earth is carried by winds in the atmosphere, and the remainder is carried by ocean currents.

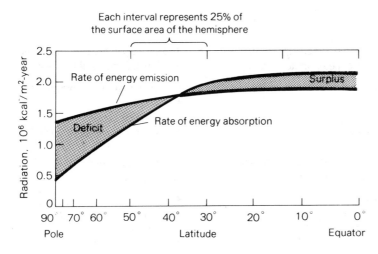

Fig. 4.10 The annual balance between incoming solar radiation and outgoing radiation from the earth. More energy is gained than lost in the tropical regions, and more energy is lost than gained in the polar regions. The latitude scale is spaced so that equal horizontal distances on the graph correspond to equal areas of the earth's surface.

B. Check your understanding

Now read the text again carefully, looking up anything you do not understand. Then answer the following questions.

1. In what ways does the atmosphere fail as an air-conditioning system?

2. What are the main purposes of an air-conditioning system?

3. What factors should be taken into account when describing climate?

4. What decides how much energy an object gives off?

5. Why is incoming energy trapped in a greenhouse?

6. What happens to the insolation given off by the sun?

7. What would the earth be like without an atmosphere?

8. Why is air near the equator hotter than air near the poles?

9. Why are desert regions hot by day but cold by night?

10. Look at Fig. 4.10. Does your country gain more energy than it loses, or lose more than it gains?

C. Increase your vocabulary

1. Look at the first paragraph and say which words have the opposite meaning to:

- very small
- strongly
- well/happily
- very hot

2. Look at paragraph 2 and say which words you could replace with:

- place
- changeability
- very great

3. Look at paragraphs 3 and 4 and say which words are used to mean:

- having more power/prevailing
- mainly
- which can be seen
- make a way into or through

4. Look at paragraph 5 and explain what the following mean:

- reradiate
- excess
- collision
- source
- in effect

5. These words occur in the remaining paragraphs. Using your dictionary, fill in the spaces with the correct form of the word given, where these exist.

Noun	Verb	Adjective
atmosphere		
	radiate	
	prevent	
absorption		
		average
region		
loss		
		present
	influence	
energy		

6. Look at paragraphs 8 and 9 again and the graph. Say what words have the opposite meaning to:

- perpendicular
- surplus
- incoming
- lost

D. Check your grammar

1. Join the following pairs of sentences together to make single sentences by using either *although* or *whereas*:

Example:
Some quartz crystals are clear. Others are milky. Although some quartz crystals are clear, others are milky.

- Clear quartz is used in jewellery. Mica is used in electrical equipment.

- Feldspar is harder than glass. It is not as hard as quartz.

- Quartz shows no cleavage. Feldspar shows good cleavage in two directions approximately at right angles.

- They have very similar properties. There are really two classes of feldspar.

- All ferromagnesian minerals are silicates of iron and magnesium. Most of them contain other metallic elements.

- The ferromagnesian minerals are dark in colour. The feldspars occur in light shades.

- Mica is a very soft mineral. It is still harder than your fingernail.

- Feldspar crystals are rectangular. Quartz crystals are six-sided prisms or pyramids.

- You can set down the colour and composition of ferromagensian minerals. No other general properties can be described.

- Calcite crystals resemble those of quartz. Calcite is a much softer mineral.

MAKING COMPARISONS

> **Do you remember?**
> It was hot*ter* in Riyadh *than* in Rio de Janeiro.
> It was *not as* hot in Rio de Janeiro *as* it was in Riyadh.
> There was *more/less* sun in Riyadh *than* in Cologne.
> The cold*est* city was . . . .

2. Look at the following temperatures round the world on a typical November day. Compare the temperatures in different parts of the world.

MIDDAY: c, cloud; d, drizzle; f, fair; fg, fog; r, rain; s, sun; sn, snow; t, thunder.

	C	F		V	F		C	F		C	F
Ajaccio	f 20	68	Cologne	c 10	50	Majorca	s 17	63	Rome	s 15	59
Akrotiri	s 20	68	C'phagn	f 8	46	Malaga	s 20	68	Salzburg	c 8	46
Alex'dria	c 21	70	Corfu	s 20	68	Malta	th 15	59	S F'risco*		
Algiers	c 18	64	Dublin	c 6	43	Melb'rne	f 14	57	Santiago*	f 18	64
Amst'dm	f 9	48	Dubrovnik	s 18	64	Mexico C*	s 22	72	S Paulo*		
Athens	s 16	61	Faro	s 20	68	Miami*			Seoul	s 11	52
Bahrain			Florence	c 12	54	Milan	c 11	52	Sing'por	d 29	84
Barbads*	f 29	84	Frankfurt	f 9	48	Montreal*	c 6	43	St'kholm	c 8	46
Barcelna	s 16	61	Funchal	c 18	64	Moscow	c 1	34	Strasb'rg	s 12	54
Beirut			Geneva	s 10	50	Munich	f 9	48	Sydney	c 17	63
Belgrade	c 5	41	Gibraltar	s 20	68	Nairobi	c 24	75	Tangier	s 19	66
Berlin	s 10	50	Helsinki	c 4	39	Naples	s 18	64	Tel aviv	c 13	55
Bermuda*	f 27	81	Hong K	c 19	66	N Delhi	s 23	73	Tenerife	f 22	72
Biarritz	f 14	57	Innsbrck	f 8	46	N York*	c 12	54	Tokyo	s 16	61
Borde'x	s 15	59	Istanbul	f 11	52	Nice	s 19	66	Toronto*	s 10	50
Boul'ne	f 12	54	Jeddah			Oslo	s 5	41	Tunis	c 17	63
Brussels	c 9	48	Jo'burg*	f 28	82	Paris	c 11	52	Valencia	f 16	61
Budapst	f 10	50	Karachi	s 28	82	Peking	s 9	48	Vanc'ver*	c 6	43
B Aires*	s 26	79	L Palmas	c 20	68	Perth	s 30	86	Venice	f 12	54
Cairo	f 21	70	Lisbon	s 15	59	Prague	f 9	48	Vienna	c 7	45
Cape Tn	f 23	73	Locarno	c 13	55	Reykjvik	f -1	30	Warsaw	c 9	48
C'blanca	s 18	64	L Angels*			Rhodes	s 19	66	Wash'ton*	c 13	55
Chicago*			Luxembg	f 7	45	Rio de J	s 26	79	Zurich	s 10	30
Ch'church	c 15	59	Madrid	s 12	54	Riyadh	s 27	81			

*denotes Monday's figures are latest available

The Times,
19 November 1986

E. Understanding a lecture

Listen to this lecture on winds. Using the information the lecturer gives you, answer the questions below. The lecture is divided into sections. Listen to each section twice.

Section 1

- What word does the lecturer use to describe the direction that wind travels?

- How does the lecturer define 'wind'?

- Is this statement correct or incorrect?

Winds are caused by pressure differences in the atmosphere. ☐

Section 2

- What causes pressure differences?

- Put these statements in the correct order:

A low-pressure zone is left.

The air also expands.

Cool air flows into the low-pressure zone.

Hot air rises.

Section 3

Use the diagram below to explain convection currents as described by the lecturer.

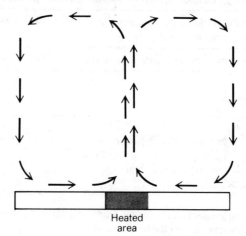

Heated area

Section 4

- "An onshore wind blows from the sea to the land. An offshore wind blows from the land to the sea."

  What causes onshore and offshore winds?

Section 5

- Are these statements correct or incorrect?

In the Northern Hemisphere a path appears to curve to the right. ☐

In the Southern Hemisphere a path appears to curve to the left. ☐

- What is the name given to this effect?

Section 6

Using the information the lecturer has given you, can you explain the illustration he is talking about?

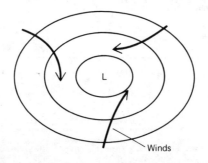

Winds

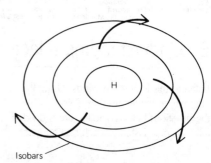

Isobars

Now listen to the lecture again. Make any notes you want. Then write a summary of the lecture. The questions you have already answered will help you.

F. Understanding a printed text (2)

Read the following text carefully, looking up anything you do not understand.

General Circulation of the Atmosphere

1   The earth as a whole is heated strongly in the equatorial belt and less strongly on either side, so we might expect to find convection currents as part of the general atmospheric circulation. Suppose for the moment that our planet did not rotate, that it was heated strongly near the equator, and that its surface was made up entirely of either land or water. On such an earth air circulation would depend exclusively on the difference in temperature between equator and poles. Air would rise along the heated equator, overflow at high altitudes toward the poles, and at low altitudes move continually from the poles back toward the equator (Fig. 4.13). People in the Northern Hemisphere would experience a steady north wind. Around the equator would be a belt of relatively low pressure, near each pole a region of high pressure.

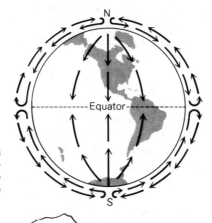

Fig. 4.13 The convectional circulation that would occur if the earth did not rotate and were heated uniformly at the equator. The arrows in the center of the diagram indicate surface winds.

2   Because the earth does rotate, the above north and south winds are deflected by the Coriolis effect into large-scale eddies that lead to a generally eastward drift in the middle latitudes of each hemisphere and a westward drift in the tropics. The principal features of the general circulation of the atmosphere are shown in Fig. 4.14. The various wind zones were important to shipping in the days of sail, as their names indicate. Thus the steady easterlies on either side of the equator became known as the *trade winds*, while the region of light, erratic wind along the equator itself, where the

The doldrums and the horse latitudes are belts of calm; the trade winds between them and the prevailing westerlies north and south of the doldrums are relatively steady

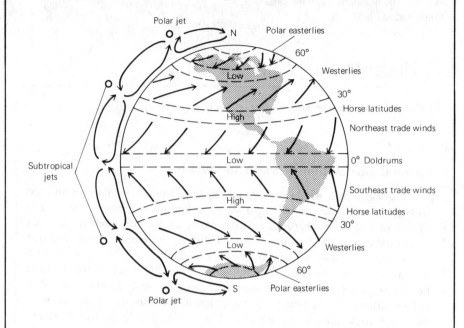

Fig. 4.14 Idealized pattern of horizontal and vertical circulation of the atmosphere. Regions of high and low pressure are indicated.

principal movement of air is upward, constitutes the *doldrums*. The *horse latitudes* that separate the trade winds in either hemisphere from the *prevailing westerlies* of the middle latitudes are also regions of light winds and are supposed to have been given their name because of the practice of throwing overboard horses carried on sailing vessels becalmed there that ran short of water.

The jet streams

3   With increasing altitude the regions of westerly winds broaden until almost the entire flow of air is west to east at the top of the troposphere. The westerly flow aloft is not uniform but contains narrow cores of high-velocity winds called *jet streams*. The jet streams form wavelike zigzag patterns around the earth that change continuously and give rise to the variable weather of the middle latitudes by their effect on air masses closer to the surface.

4   At any given time the circulation near the surface is more complicated than the pattern given in Fig. 4.14. An important factor is the presence of large seasonal low- and high-pressure cells caused by unequal heating due to the irregular distribution of landmasses and sea masses (Fig. 4.15). Smaller, short-lived cells also occur which profoundly affect local weather conditions.

Air Masses, Cyclones, and Anticyclones

5   Day-to-day weather is more variable in the middle latitudes than anywhere else on earth. If we visit central Mexico or Hawaii, in the belt of the northeast trades, we find that one day follows another with hardly any change in temperature, moisture, or wind direction, whereas in nearly all parts of

the continental United States abrupt changes in weather are commonplace. The reason for this variability lies in the movement of warm and cold air masses and of storms derived from them through the belt of the westerlies.

6   In the northern part of the westerly belt an irregular boundary separates air moving generally northward from the horse latitudes and air moving southward from the polar regions. Great tongues of cold air at times sweep down over North America, and at other times warm air from the tropics extends far northward. The cold air is ultimately warmed and the warm air cooled, but a large body of air can maintain nearly its original temperature and humidity for days or weeks. These huge tongues of air, or isolated bodies of air detached from them, are the *air masses* of meteorology. The kind of air in an air mass depends on its source: a mass formed over northern Canada is cold and dry, one from the North Atlantic or North Pacific is cold and humid, one from the Gulf of Mexico warm and humid, and so on.

The motion of air masses determines middle-latitude weather

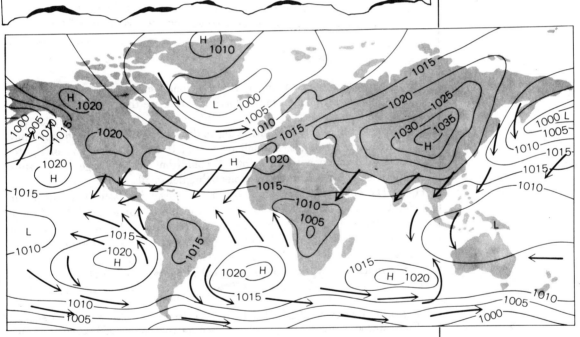

Fig. 4.15 Average January sea-level pressures (in millibars) and winds. High- and low-pressure systems are indicated. The black lines that join points which have the same pressure are called isobars.

7   Weather systems associated with air masses are usually several hundred to a thousand or more miles across and move from west to east. At the center of a *cyclone* the air pressure is low, and as air rushes in toward it the moving air is deflected toward the right in the Northern Hemisphere and toward the left in the Southern because of the Coriolis effect. As a result cyclonic winds blow in a counterclockwise spiral in the Northern Hemisphere and in a clockwise spiral in the Southern Hemisphere. An *anticyclone* is centered on a high-pressure region from which air moves outward. The Coriolis effect

Cyclones are centered on low-pressure regions, anticyclones on high-pressure ones

therefore causes anticyclonic winds to blow in a clockwise spiral in the Northern Hemisphere and in a counterclockwise spiral in the Southern Hemisphere. These spirals are conspicuous in cloud formations photographed from earth satellites.

8   A cyclone is a region of low pressure, and air flowing into one rises in an upward spiral. The rising air cools and its moisture content condenses into clouds. As a rule, cyclones bring unstable weather conditions with clouds, rain, strong shifting winds, and abrupt temperature changes (Fig. 4.17). An anticyclone is a region of high pressure, and air flows out of it in a downward spiral. The descent warms the air and its relative humidity accordingly drops, hence condensation does not occur. The weather associated with anticyclones is usually settled and pleasant with clear skies and little wind.

The polar front

9   Middle-latitude cyclones originate at the *polar front*, which is the boundary between the cold polar air mass and the warmed air mass adjacent to it. It is common for a kink to develop in this front with a wedge of warm air protruding into the cold air mass. This produces a low-pressure region which moves eastward as a cyclone. The eastern side of the warm-air wedge

Warm and cold fronts

is a *warm front* since warm air moves in to replace cold air in its path; the western side is a *cold front* since cold air replaces warm air (Fig. 4.18).

10   As warm air rises along an inclined frontal surface it is cooled and part of its moisture condenses out. Clouds and rain are therefore associated with both kinds of fronts (Fig. 4.19). A cold frontal surface is generally steeper, since cold air is actively burrowing under warm air, and the temperature difference is greater, so rainfall on a cold front is heavier and of shorter duration than on a warm front. A cold front with a large temperature difference is often marked by violent thundersqualls.

11   The cold front associated with a cyclone moves faster than the warm front, and eventually it overtakes the warm front to force the wedge of warm air upwards (Fig. 4.20). The formation of such an *occluded front* is the last stage in the evolution of a cyclone, which soon afterward disappears. The total life span of a middle-latitude cyclone may be as little as a few hours or as much as a week, though the usual range is 3 to 5 days.

Fig. 4.20 Life cycle of a middle-latitude cyclone in the Northern Hemisphere. Conventional weather-map symbols are used for cold, warm, and occluded fronts.

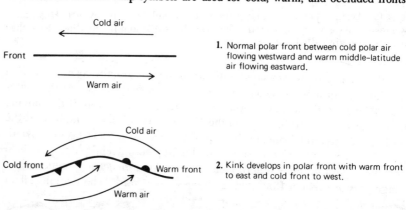

Cold air

Front

Warm air

1. Normal polar front between cold polar air flowing westward and warm middle-latitude air flowing eastward.

Cold air

Cold front   Warm front

Warm air

2. Kink develops in polar front with warm front to east and cold front to west.

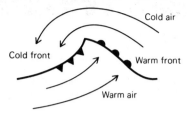

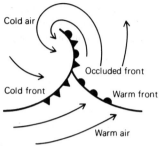

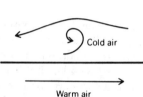

Cold air

Warm air

3. Mature cyclone with characteristic counter-clockwise circulation and well-developed warm and cold fronts.

4. The cold front has begun to overtake the warm front to form an occluded front in which the warm air wedge is forced upward to leave cold air at the surface.

5. All the warm air in the wedge has been replaced by cold air at the surface in the final stage of decay; the remaining whirl of cold air will soon disappear.

G. Check your understanding

1. Look at the first section (paragraphs 1–4) and explain in your own words the terms:

- trade winds
- doldrums
- horse latitudes
- prevailing westerlies
- jet streams

2. Look at paragraphs 5 and 6 and say which words have the same meaning as:

- stretches
- in the end

- on its/their own
- usually

3. Look at paragraphs 7 and 8:

- Can you explain the difference between a *cyclone* and an *anticyclone*?

4. Look at paragraph 9 and say what the following words refer to:

- it (line 3, first word)
- this (line 4)
- its (line 6)

H. Understanding discourse

Listen to the lecturer telling you the procedure to follow if you want to use a laboratory on your own. Note down the procedure you must follow.

_____

_____

_____

_____

_____

_____

UNIT 7

THE OCEANS

A. Understanding a printed text (1)

The following text will introduce you to the topic of the **oceans**. Look at the way it is divided into sections and paragraphs. Pay attention to the headings and notes in the margins, and to the illustrations and captions.

Now look at these questions:

1. What are the most important words used to describe ocean basins?

2. What does Fig. 5.1 illustrate?
3. What is the second section about?

Read the passage through and find the answers to the questions. Remember, you do not have to understand every word to answer them.

Ocean Basins

Continental shelf

1 Each of the world's oceans lies in a vast basin bounded by continental landmasses. Typically an ocean bottom slopes gradually downward from the shore to an average depth of 130 m or so before starting to drop more rapidly (Fig. 5.1). The average width of this *continental shelf* is 65 km, but it ranges from hardly anything off such mountainous coasts as the western coast of South America to over 1,000 km off the low arctic coasts of the Eurasian landmass. The North, Irish, and Baltic Seas are part of the European continental shelf, while the Grand Banks off Newfoundland are part of the North American shelf. The total area of the continental shelves exceeds that of South America.

The steep continental slope marks the true margin of a continent

An increase in gradient marks the transition from the continental shelf to the steeper *continental slope,* which after a fall of perhaps 2 km joins the *abyssal plain* of the ocean floor via the gentle *continental rise.*

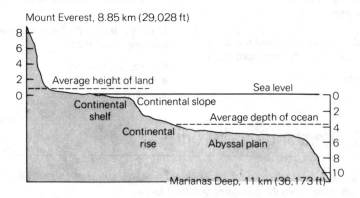

Fig. 5.1 Profile of the earth's surface. The vertical scale is greatly exaggerated; the average gradient of most continental slopes is only a few degrees, for instance. Heights and depths are in kilometers.

2   The ocean basins average 3.7 km in depth, while the continents average only about 0.8 km in height above sea level. The deepest known point of the oceans, 11 km below the surface, is found in the Marianas Trench southwest of Guam in the Pacific; by contrast, Mt. Everest is only 80 percent as high above sea level. If the earth were smooth, it would be covered with a layer of water perhaps 2.4 km thick, but it seems likely that the oceans have always been confined to more or less distinct basins and presumably will continue to be.

3   The topography of the ocean floor, like that of the continents, is marked by mountain ranges and valleys, isolated volcanic peaks and vast plains, many of them rivaling or exceeding in size their terrestrial counterparts. The Hawaiian Islands, for instance, are volcanoes that rise as much as 30,000 ft above the ocean floor, about half of their altitude being above sea level. Less conspicuous from the surface is the Mid-Atlantic Ridge, an immense submarine mountain range that extends from Iceland past the tip of South America before swinging into the Indian Ocean. Such islands as the Azores, Ascension Island, and Tristan da Cunha are all that protrude from the ocean of this ridge.

Topography of the ocean floor

4   A considerable amount of water is stored as ice in the form of the glaciers and ice caps which cover one-tenth the land area of the earth. About 90 percent of this ice is located in the Antarctic ice cap, about 9 percent in the Greenland ice cap, and the remaining 1 percent in the various glaciers of the world. If suddenly melted, the ice would raise sea level by perhaps 60 m, which would flood a large proportion of continental land areas. (By comparison, if all the water vapor in the atmosphere were condensed, sea level would go up by only about 3 cm.) Over a long period of time the rise in sea level would be reduced by about one-third by changes in the levels of the continents and the ocean floors brought about by the changes in the weights they have to bear.

The Antarctic ice cap contains most of the world's permanent ice

Composition

5   Seawater has a salt content, or *salinity*, that averages 3.5 percent. The composition of seawater in terms of ions is shown in Fig. 5.2. An ion, as mentioned earlier, is an atom or group of atoms that has an electric charge. Salts break up into ions when they dissolve in water; thus table salt, NaCl (sodium chloride), yields Na^+ and Cl^- ions. The latter ions, in fact, account for over 85 percent of the dissolved material in seawater. The salinity of seawater varies around the world, but the proportions of the various ions are virtually the same everywhere.

The salinity of seawater averages 3.5 percent; most of the ions present are Na^+ and Cl^-

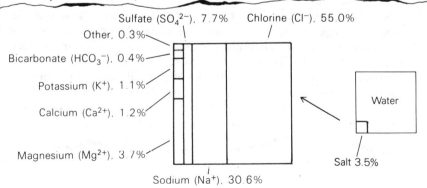

Fig. 5.2 The composition of seawater. In the open ocean the total salt content varies about an average of 3.5 percent but the relative proportions of the various ions are constant. (Percentages given are by weight.)

6   Most of the earth's surface water probably appeared when the young earth assumed its present internal structure. The water was liberated from the rocks of the interior and took with it the same ions found in seawater today: the oceans have always been salty. Since then, additional salts have continually been added to the oceans in the various ways illustrated in Fig. 5.3. However, seawater salinity has not change by very much because of the action of various mechanisms that remove salts from the oceans. One of these mechanisms is quite direct, the loss of salts to the atmosphere when wind blows spray off wave tops; the resulting salt particles serve as precipitation nuclei, and a substantial amount falls on land in rain and snow. Another mechanism is the incorporation

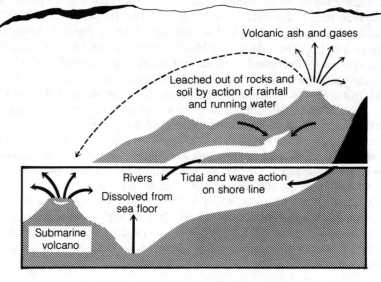

Volcanic ash and gases

Leached out of rocks and soil by action of rainfall and running water

Rivers

Dissolved from sea floor

Tidal and wave action on shore line

Submarine volcano

Fig. 5.3   The various ways in which salts are added to seawater today. The chief source is rock from the interior that wells up in rifts in the ocean floors.

of various compounds, notably calcium carbonate and silicon dioxide, in the shells of marine organisms, which eventually form part of the sediments that coat the ocean floors.

7   Seawater contains dissolved gases as well as salt ions. Because of the constant exchange of gases at the sea-air boundary, the uppermost layer of the oceans is *saturated* with atmospheric gases: there is an equilibrium in which as much gas of any kind leaves the water as enters it. Just below the surface layer, though, the photosynthetic activities of plant life lead to a disproportionately greater oxygen concentration. Deep in the ocean, there is relatively little oxygen because animal life there consumes oxygen and there is not enough sunlight for plants to produce more in photosynthesis.

Seawater has always been salty

Carbon dioxide in the oceans

8   Only a fraction of the carbon dioxide in the ocean remains in the form of carbon dioxide (CO_2) molecules. Most of it reacts with water to form carbonate (CO_3^{2-}) and bicarbonate (HCO_3^-) ions. Because water can hold much more carbon dioxide in the form of HCO_3^- and CO_3^{2-} ions than in the form of CO_2 molecules, the total carbon dioxide content of the oceans is far greater than its rather low (0.03 percent by volume) concentration in the atmosphere would suggest. It is estimated that there are 1.3×10^{14} tons of carbon dioxide in the oceans of the world, and the continual exchange of CO_2 between the atmosphere and the oceanic reservoir probably involves more CO_2 than the exchange between the atmosphere and the biologic reservoir of plant and animal life.

B. Check your understanding

Now read the text again carefully, looking up anything you do not understand. Then answer the following questions.

1. How wide are continental shelves?

2. What differentiates the continental slope from the continental rise?

3. What is the abyssal plain?

4. What is the Marianas Trench?

5. What is the similarity between the ocean floor and the land?

6. What would happen if all the ice in the world melted?

7. What is salinity?

8. Where did the earth's surface water come from?

9. What does seawater contain in addition to salt ions?

10. Why is there more oxygen below the surface layer of the sea?

C. Increase your vocabulary

1. These words occur in the text. Using your dictionary, fill in the spaces with the correct form of the word given:

Noun	Verb	Adjective
		deep
width		
height		

2. Look at the first paragraph again. Using words from it, complete the following:

- Chile is a country that is _____ on the west by the Pacific Ocean. Because the coast is _____ there is hardly any continental shelf. Chile is, of course, part of the South American _____.

3. Now look at paragraph 2 and say which words have the opposite meaning to:

- rough
- shallowest

4. Now look at paragraph 3. These words are used in association with mountains. Can you explain them?

- range
- peak
- ridge

5. In the same paragraph, which words have the same meaning as:

- vast
- stick up from
- of the land

6. Now look at paragraph 4. Two words are used to describe ice formations. Can you explain them?

- glacier
- ice cap

7. Now look at paragraph 5 and then explain the following words:

- dissolve
- proportions

8. Now look at paragraph 6. What words are used to mean:

- a living being
- of or in the inside
- going on all the time without stopping
- the inside of something
- in the end
- large; considerable

9. Now look at paragraphs 7 and 8 and explain the following:

- equilibrium
- concentration
- reservoir

D. Check your grammar

ASKING QUESTIONS

Can you ask questions in a way that makes sure that you get the information you want? And that you understand the answers? Look at the table below. It is blank. When it is complete, it will show you the relationship between wind speed and the state of the sea surface in open water. The teacher has the information you need to complete the table. Ask the questions you need to ask and note down the answers. Start by asking about the headings.

E. Understanding a lecture

Listen to this lecture on ocean waves. Using the information the lecturer gives you, answer the questions below. The lecture is divided into sections. Listen to each section twice.

Section 1

- Complete the following statement, choosing the correct ending:

  The lecturer tells the students that:

  they must look at the handout ☐

  they must not look at the handout ☐

  they can look at the handout if they want to ☐

- What word does the lecturer use to describe the top of a wave?

- What differences between a ripple and a true wave does the lecturer describe?

- Which three factors does the lecturer say govern the height of waves? Complete these statements:

  _____
  , the higher the waves.

  _____
  , the higher the waves.

  _____
  , the higher the waves.

Section 2

- What word does the lecturer use to describe the *greatest* height of a wave?

- Complete the following table, using the figures the lecturer gives you:

	Wind speed	Wave height	Duration of wind	Distance travelled
Example 1				
Example 2				

Section 3

- What phenomenon is the lecturer talking about?

- Are these statements correct or incorrect?

  The direction of the wind decides how waves approach the shore. ☐

  Waves out to sea travel in the same direction as those approaching the shore. ☐

  Waves approaching the shore are parallel to the shoreline. ☐

Section 4

- Oblique means _____

- Are these statements correct or incorrect?

  A wave increases its speed when it meets shallow water. ☐

  Friction with the sea bottom is what slows a wave down. ☐

  A wave front means a line of waves. ☐

  A wave front swings towards the shore because part of it is moving more slowly than the rest. ☐

- Now listen to the lecture again. Make any notes you want. Then write a summary to explain the phenomenon of refraction. The questions you have already answered will help you.

F. Understanding a printed text (2)

Read the following text carefully, looking up anything you do not understand.

The Tides

1   That there is a relationship of some kind between the moon and the rhythm of the tides was known even in ancient times. Dwellers beside the ocean have been aware for thousands of years of such aspects of tidal behavior as that at new moon and full moon the difference between high water and low water is larger than it is when only half the moon's disk is visible.

Origin of the tides

2   Not until Newton was the cause of the tide finally ascribed to the gravitational attraction of the moon and, to a smaller extent, of the sun as well. A complete explanation is rather involved, but the basic argument is not hard to follow. Water at A in Fig. 5.8 is closest to the moon, and is heaped up by its gravitational pull. Water at B is farthest from the moon, and is least attracted by it; this water tends to be left behind, so to speak, as the earth is pulled away from under it due to the revolution of the earth and moon about their common center of mass. (The earth's pull on the moon, which causes it to move in an orbit around the earth, has a counterpart in the moon's pull on the earth, which in response moves in an orbit around the moon, although a much smaller one. Earth and moon may be thought of as the two ends of a dumbbell that is rotating about its balance point, which happens to lie within the earth about 4,700 km from the center. It is this center of mass that moves in an orbit around the sun.)

Two tidal cycles occur each day at a given place

3   Solid rock resists the bulging effect to a large extent (though there *are* detectable tides in the earth's crust), but the fluid ocean responds easily. Water is heaped up on the sides of the earth facing and directly opposite the moon, and is drawn away from other parts of the earth. As the earth rotates on its axis, the water bulges are held in position by the moon. The earth, so to speak, moves under the bulges, and a given point on its surface therefore experiences two high tides and two low tides per day.

4   Because the moon is much closer to the earth than the sun is, the differences in the forces it exerts on different parts of the earth are greater than those in the forces exerted by the sun, even though the forces themselves are stronger in the case of the sun. For this reason the moon is chiefly responsible for the tides, with the solar influence limited to modifying the tidal range depending on the relative position of the sun with respect to the earth and moon. About twice a month, when sun, moon, and earth are in a straight line, solar tides are added to lunar tides to form the unusually high (and low) *spring* tides; when the line between moon and earth is perpendicular to that

Spring and neap tides

Fig. 5.8 Explanation of the tides. The moon's attraction is greatest at *A*, least at *B*.

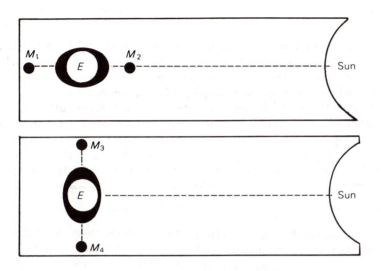

Fig. 5.9 Variation of the tides. Spring tides are produced when the moon is at M_1 or M_2, neap tides when the moon is at M_3 or M_4.

between sun and earth, the tide-raising forces oppose each other and tides are the *neap* tides whose range is small (Fig. 5.9).

5   The earth makes a complete rotation on its axis once every 24 h, but the interval between successive high tides is 12 h 25 min instead of 12 h. The reason follows from the moon's orbital motion around the earth. The moon revolves around the earth in the same direction as the earth's rotation and takes 29.5 days to circle the earth relative to the sun; that is, 29.5 days elapse from new moon to new moon. Thus the moon is directly overhead a certain place on the earth 24 h/29.5 days = 0.81 h *later* each day than the day before, which is 50 min. There are two tides a day, and half of 24 h 50 min is the observed 12 h 25 min interval between them.

Earth

Moon

Fig. 5.10 The tidal bulges are dragged ahead of the moon by the earth's rotation. The friction between the bulges and the earth slows the earth's rotation on its axis, while the gravitational pull of the bulges speeds up the moon's revolution in its orbit. The effect is considerably exaggerated in the figure.

6   The earth does not rotate smoothly beneath the tidal bulges but tries to carry them around with it. The moon's attraction prevents them from being dragged very far, but the line between the bulges is somewhat inclined to the line between earth and moon (Fig. 5.10). In this position the moon holds the bulges firmly, and the upraised water drags back on the earth as it rotates. Friction between water and rotating earth is not very great in the open ocean, but along irregular coasts it may be considerable. The effect of the friction is, of course, to slow the earth's rotation; the tidal bulges act like huge but inefficient brake bands clamped on opposite sides of the spinning planet.

The length of the day is increasing slowly because of tidal friction

7   In other words, because of tidal friction the day is slowly growing longer. Verification of this effect has come from records of ancient eclipses, among other sources. Using the day's present length, astronomers can calculate precisely when and where eclipses have occurred in the past. These calculations do not agree with the observations recorded by ancient Egyptian and Babylonian astronomers, the discrepancies being greatest for the oldest eclipses. Calculated and observed positions, however, agree well if the slow increase in the day's length is considered. The rate of increase is very small: the time between sunrise and sunrise is longer today by $\frac{1}{1,000}$ s than it was 100 years ago, long by $\frac{1}{50}$ s than 2,000 years ago.

G. Check your understanding

1. Look at paragraphs 1 and 2 and say which words are used to mean:

- a round surface that appears to be flat
- a regular rise and fall
- the path followed by a heavenly body round another
- something that closely corresponds to another

2. Look at paragraph 3 and say whether these statements are correct or incorrect:

- Rock does not correspond at all to the gravitational pull of the moon. ☐

- Water only piles up on the side of the earth facing the moon. ☐

- Water bulges are held in position because the earth rotates. ☐

3. Look at paragraph 4 and say whether these statements are correct or incorrect:

- The sun exerts some influence on the earth's tides. ☐

- The moon is mainly responsible for the earth's tides because it is nearer. ☐

4. In paragraph 4 two terms are used to describe different kinds of tide.

- What are the two terms?
- Can you explain the difference between the two?

5. Look at paragraphs 5 and 6 again:

- How many words in these two paragraphs describe movement of one kind or another?
- Write a sentence of your own with each word you have found.

6. Look at paragraph 7 again and explain the words:

- verification
- eclipse

H. Understanding discourse

Listen to a lecturer giving instructions to some students. Answer the questions below.

1. What is the subject of next week's lectures?

_____

2. The two books to be read are

Title_____

Author_____

Chapter_____

Pages_____

Title_____

Author_____

Chapter_____

Pages_____

3. The article to be read is

Journal_____

Volume_____

Title_____

Author_____

4. What must the students be able to describe before the next lecture?

_____

UNIT

8

THE CLIMATE

A. Understanding a printed text (1)

The following text will introduce you to the topic of the **climate**. Look at the way it is divided into sections and paragraphs. Pay attention to the headings and notes in the margins, and to the illustrations and captions.

Now look at these questions:

1. What two elements determine climate?
2. What are the five principal categories of climate?

3. In how many ways do the oceans influence climate?
4. What are these ways?
5. What does Fig. 5.12 illustrate?

Read the passage through and find the answers to the questions. Remember, you do not have to understand every word to answer them.

There are five principal types of climate

CLIMATE

1. The climate of a region refers both to its average weather over a period of years and to the typical amounts by which the various weather elements vary during each day and during each year. The most significant weather elements in determining climate are temperature and precipitation. Climates differ considerably around the world, ranging from the tropics where there is no winter to the polar regions where there is hardly any summer. The belts in each hemisphere between the tropics and the polar regions were once classed simply as the temperate zones. A more realistic appraisal shows that at least five broad types of climate can be distinguished, each with a number of subdivisions.

Climate Classification

2. The present system of climate classification was devised in 1918 by Wladimir Köppen. The principal categories in the Köppen system are:

A Tropical rainy climates. The average monthly temperature goes below 18°C (64.4°F) and there is little seasonal variation. Annual rainfall exceeds the water lost by evaporation.

B Dry climates. The water lost by evaporation exceeds that brought by precipitation.

C Warm temperature rainy climates. There are distinct summer and winter seasons, with the average temperature of the coldest month lower than 18°C (64.4°F) but higher than −3°C (26.6°F).

D Cool snow-forest climates. The average temperature of the coldest month is lower than −3°C (26.6°F) and that of the warmest month is higher than 10°C (50°F).

E Polar climates. The average temperature of the warmest month remains below 10°C (50°F). Trees do not thrive in such climates.

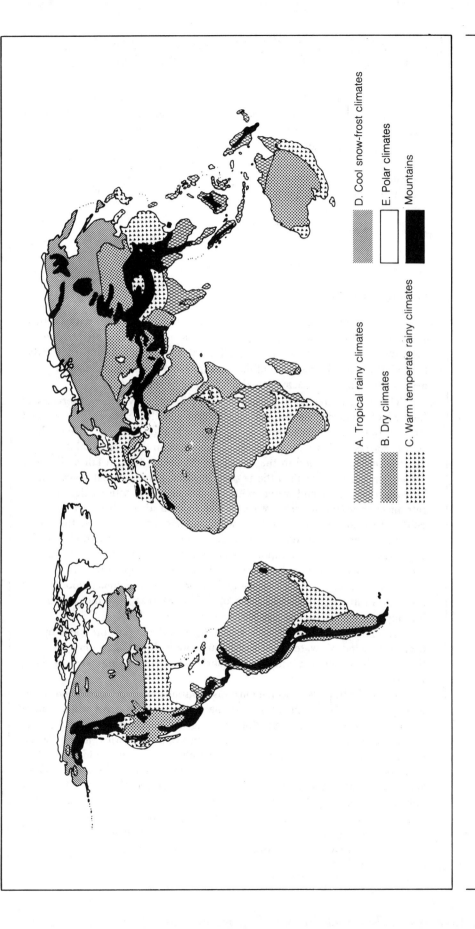

A. Tropical rainy climates

B. Dry climates

C. Warm temperate rainy climates

D. Cool snow-frost climates

E. Polar climates

Mountains

3 Figure 5.11 shows the general distribution of the above climates around the world. It is worth emphasizing that a complete climate classification would include factors not considered here, for instance the distribution of rainfall during the year: there is a big difference between a type C climate which is moist all year round and one in which the rainfall is concentrated in one season. Another aspect omitted from Fig. 5.11 is the sometimes considerable local variation in climate within a given climate band that local conditions, such as the presence of a mountain range, can produce.

Ocean Currents

4 The existence of different climates is due to the variation with latitude and season of the solar radiation arriving at the earth. This affects climate both directly, through the heating effect of the radiation, and indirectly, through the general circulation of the atmosphere that results. A secondary but nevertheless important element is the influence of the oceans.

The oceans act as heat reservoirs that moderate the climates of adjoining land areas

5 The oceans affect climate in two ways. First, they act as reservoirs of heat which moderate the temperature extremes of the seasons. In spring and summer the oceans are cooler than the regions bordering them, since the heat they absorb is dissipated in a greater volume than in the case of solid, opaque land. The heat retained in the ocean depths means that in fall and winter the oceans are warmer than the regions bordering them. Heat flows readily between moving air and water; with a sufficient temperature difference, the rate of energy transfer from warm water to cold air (or from warm air to cold water) can exceed the rate at which solar energy arrives at the top of the atmosphere. With no such heat reservoir nearby, continental interiors experience lower winter temperatures and higher summer temperatures than those of coastal districts. In Canada, for instance, temperatures in the city of Victoria on the Pacific Coast range from an average January minimum of 36°F to an average July maximum of 68°F, whereas in Winnipeg, in the interior, the corresponding figures are −8°F and 80°F.

6 Also influencing climate are surface drifts in the oceans produced by the friction of wind on water. Such drifts are much slower than movements in the atmosphere, with the fastest normal surface currents having speeds of about 7 mi/h.

Surface ocean currents are caused by winds

7 The wind-impelled surface currents parallel to a large extent the major wind systems. The northeast and southeast trade winds drive water before them westward along the equator, forming the *equatorial current.* In the Atlantic Ocean this current runs head on into South America, in the Pacific into the East Indies. At each of these points the current divides into two parts, one flowing south and the other north. Moving away from the equator along the continental margins, these currents at length come under the influence of the westerlies, which drive them eastward across the oceans. Thus

Gyres

gigantic whirlpools called *gyres* are set up in both Atlantic and Pacific Oceans on either side of the equator (Fig. 5.12). Many complexities are produced in the four great gyres by islands, continental projections, and undersea mountains and valleys.

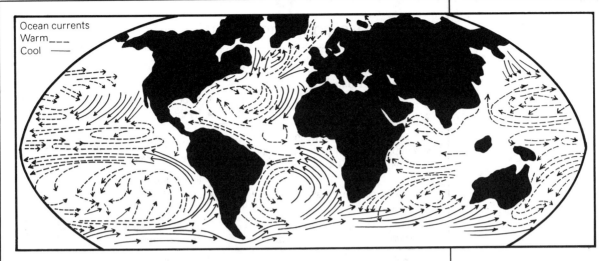

Fig. 5.12 Principal ocean currents of the world. Warm currents are shown by the dotted arrows, and cool currents by the black ones.

8   Currents also occur deep in the ocean, though their speeds are usually slower than those of surface currents. In the polar regions of both hemispheres cold water sinks because of its greater density and flows toward the equator several miles below the surface. These cold currents keep tropical waters cooler than they otherwise would be, and they also bring oxygen to the lower depths of the ocean which enables plant and animal life to occur there.

9   Thus the oceans, besides acting as water reservoirs for the earth's atmosphere, play a direct part in temperature control—both by preventing abrupt temperature changes in lands along their borders and by aiding the winds, through the motion of ocean currents, in their distribution of heat and cold over the surface of the earth.

B. Check your understanding

Now read the text again carefully, looking up anything you do not understand. Then answer the following questions:

1. What part of the world has no winter?

2. What was the term given to the belts between the tropics and the polar regions?

3. What is the average monthly temperature in a tropical climate?

4. What category does your country come in?

5. In what climate do trees not grow?

6. What aspects are not included in the climate classification?

7. Why are there different climates?

8. What is the speed of the surface drifts in the ocean?

9. What is a gyre?

10. What influence do cold currents have on tropical waters?

C. Increase your vocabulary

1. Look at paragraphs 1 and 2 again. What words are used to mean:

- free from the extremes of heat and cold
- thought/worked out
- make a difference between
- groups into which something is put
- succeed; grow well

2. Look at paragraph 3 again. Complete the following table:

Noun	Verb
emphasis	
	distribute
	classify
concentration	
difference	

3. Look at paragraphs 4 and 5 and say which words have the same meaning as:

- all the same
- have an influence on

- kept
- autumn
- to be greater/more than
- by the sea

4. Look at paragraph 7 again and say what these words refer to:

- line 4: this
- line 5: these

5. Look at paragraph 8 again and say what these words refer to:

- line 1: their
- line 3: its
- line 6: there

6. Look at paragraph 9 again and say what words have the same meaning as:

- in addition to
- sudden
- helping

D. Check your grammar

DEFINING

> **Do you remember?**
> The Beaufort Scale is a scale *which* is used to describe wind speed.
> Newton was the man *who* discovered the laws of gravity.

1. Define each of the words given below, like this:

Example: The Beaufort Scale
    The Beaufort Scale is a scale which is used to describe wind speed.

- The equatorial current

_____

- A gyre

_____

- Ferromagnesian minerals

_____

- Wladimir Köppen

_____

- A continental shelf

_____

- The abyssal plain

_____

- A neap tide

_____

- Volcanic ash

_____

- Crystals

_____

- Igneous rocks

_____

2. You can often make the opposites of words by using the prefixes dis-, un-, and in-. Make the opposites of these words using those prefixes:

- distinct
- successful
- similar
- significant
- important

- possess
- conspicuous
- changed
- soluble
- proportionate

E. Understanding a lecture

Listen to this lecture on different kinds of climate. Note down the main characteristics of the climates described by the lecturer. The lecture is divided into sections. Listen to each section twice.

Section 1—————————————
- Climate_____

  Wet/dry_____

  Rain?_____

  Winds_____

  Temperature_____

  Other notes_____

_____

Sections 2 and 3————————————————————————————————

• Climate_____

  Wet/dry_____

  Rain?_____

  Winds_____

  Temperature_____

  Other notes_____

  _____

Section 4————————————————————————————————————

• Climate_____

  Wet/dry_____

  Rain?_____

  Winds_____

  Temperature_____

  Other notes_____

  _____

Section 5————————————————————————————————————

• Climate_____

  Wet/dry_____

  Rain?_____

  Winds_____

  Temperature_____

  Other notes_____

  _____

Now write a summary, using the notes you have made. You may find it helpful to look back at Understanding a Printed Text (1) on pages 50–55 when you write your summary.

F. Understanding a printed text (2)

Read the following text carefully, looking up anything you do not understand.

Climatic Change

1   Weather we expect to vary, both from day to day and from season to season. Nor are we surprised when one year has a colder winter or a drier summer than the one before. Less familiar are changes in climate. Even though climate represents averages in weather conditions over periods of, say, 20 or 30 years, there is abundant evidence that it, too, is not constant but instead undergoes quite marked fluctuations over long spans of time. The most dramatic such fluctuations were the *ice ages* of the past, which we shall examine in Chap. 11.

Climates are subject to long-term change

2   The last ice age reached its peak about 20,000 years ago when huge ice sheets hundreds of meters thick in places covered much of Europe and North America. Then the ice began to retreat and climates became progressively less severe; in a period of 12,000 years the average annual temperature of central Europe rose from −4°C to +9°C (24°F to 48°F). By about 6,000 years ago average temperatures were a few degrees higher than those of today. A time of declining temperatures then set in, reaching a minimum in Europe between 2,500 and 3,000 years ago.

3   A gradual warming up followed that came to a peak between 1,200 and 800 years ago; so generally fine were climatic conditions then that the Vikings established flourishing colonies in Iceland and Greenland from which they went on to visit North America. The subsequent deterioration led to cool summers, exceptionally cold winters, and extensive freezing of the Arctic Sea from 700 to 300 years ago. So extreme was the weather about 350 years ago that it has been called the "Little Ice Age." Greenland became a much less attractive place than formerly and the colony there disappeared, the coast of Iceland was surrounded by ice for several months per year (in contrast to a few weeks per year today), and glaciers advanced farther across alpine landscapes than ever before or since in recorded history.

The Little Ice Age

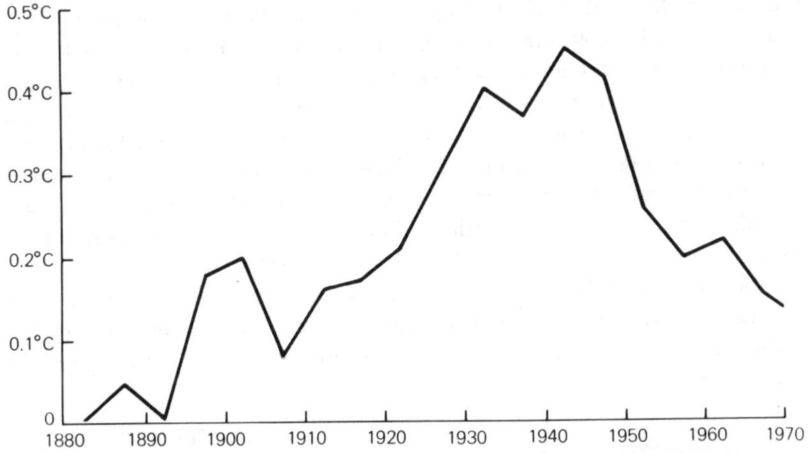

Fig. 5.13 Changes in worldwide average annual temperatures since 1880. Five-year averages are plotted.

4   During the last century a trend toward higher temperatures became evident which has led to a marked shrinkage of the world's glaciers. In the first half of this century especially pronounced temperature increases took place whose most noticeable consequences were milder winters in the higher latitudes. In Spitzbergen, for instance, January temperatures averaged from 1920 to 1940 were nearly 8°C (14°F) higher than those averaged from 1900 to 1920, and Greenland became less inhospitable than before.

5   Alas, these balmy conditions seem to have peaked about 1945, and since then the worldwide average annual temperature has been falling steadily (Fig. 5.13). The total drop in the past 30 years has been less than 0.5°C, which does not seem like very much, but the effects have been dramatic. What has happened has been a shift toward the equator of the various wind and climatic zones. In the Northern Hemisphere this shift has had a variety of effects. Siberia is growing colder as the polar front moves south. The northern rim of Africa, formerly in the dry zone of the horse latitudes, now receives unaccustomed rain as the cyclonic weather systems of the westerlies sometimes sweep over it. The horse latitudes have moved farther south, depriving vast areas of sub-Sahara Africa, the Middle East, India, and southern Asia of the moist tropical air that formerly brought them abundant rain. Famines have been the result. In North America, the pattern of air flow has changed so as to bring colder winters and more precipitation to western states while eastern ones have warmer winters.

Origin of Climatic Change

6   What causes climates to change? So many different factors influence climate that there is no shortage of possible explanations. One train of thought blames mankind for the temperature fluctuations of Fig. 5.13. The initial temperature rise is attributed to an increase in the carbon dioxide content of the atmosphere. Both the biologic and oceanic cycles are, on the average, balanced in their consumption and production of carbon dioxide. But there are also sources of carbon dioxide that have no absorption processes to counter their effects. The most significant of these sources is the burning of coal and oil by man to produce heat for dwellings and mechanical energy for industry and transportation. At present our chimneys and exhaust pipes pour about 12 billion tons of carbon dioxide each year into the atmosphere, and this rate is rapidly increasing. Since 1880 the carbon dioxide content of the atmosphere has gone up by 12 percent (Fig. 5.14). Despite the relatively small proportion of carbon dioxide in the atmosphere—only 330 parts per million—it is a most significant constituent because of its ability to absorb solar energy reradiated by the earth and thus to contribute to the greenhouse effect that provides energy to the atmosphere.

7   The cooling of the atmosphere since 1945 must have a different explanation since the carbon dioxide content has continued to increase. The culprit here is thought by some scientists to be dust at high altitudes which scatters a portion of the incoming sunlight back into space. The chief natural source of airborne dust is volcanic eruptions. Man's contribution comes from the chimneys of industry, large-scale burning of tropical forests to clear land for agriculture, and soil particles blown away during mechanical cultivation. There is no question that a sufficiently large increase in atmospheric dust would lead to the observed general cooling of the atmosphere—but just how large an increase is needed and whether it has in fact occurred are not known, nor are the relative importances of the different dust sources.

8   Another point of view attributes climatic change to variations in the solar energy arriving at the top of the atmosphere, not to events within the atmosphere. (Of course, the carbon dioxide and dust contents of the atmosphere play a role in climate: the issue is which influences are primary and which are secondary.) The sun's radiation is not constant but fluctuates through the 11-year sunspot cycle (Chap. 13), and a number of weather phenomena apparently follow a similar cycle. Perhaps there are long-term variations in solar output as well. Also, periodic changes in the earth's orbit bring it exceptionally close to and far from the sun from time to time. But does the radiation reaching the earth vary enough when this happens to produce the drastic climatic changes known to have taken place in the past, notably the ice ages? The puzzle of climatic change remains one of the most challenging in earth science.

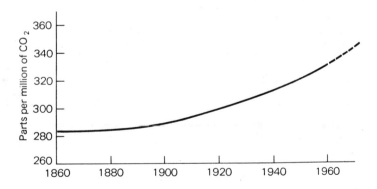

Fig. 5.14 The carbon dioxide content of the atmosphere since 1860. The increase is believed to be largely due to the combustion of coal and oil.

G. Check your understanding

1. Look at the first paragraph and say whether these statements are correct or incorrect:

- People do not expect the weather to change from year to year. ☐
- Everybody knows very well that climates change. ☐
- The ice ages marked a change in climate. ☐

2. Look at paragraph 2 and say which words have the opposite meaning to:

- advance
- rising
- maximum

3. Look at paragraph 3 and say which words have the same meaning as:

- worsening
- widespread
- previously

4. Look at paragraph 4 and then explain the words:

- shrinkage
- pronounced

5. Look at paragraph 5 and say what effect the drop in temperature has had on:

- the Northern Hemisphere
- the northern rim of Africa
- the Middle East
- North America

6. Look at the second section (paragraphs 6–8) and complete the following statements correctly:

- Some people believe the temperature fluctuations shown in Fig. 5.13 are caused by:

  the biologic and oceanic cycles ☐

  an increase in carbon dioxide ☐

  people ☐

- The carbon dioxide content of the atmosphere is:

  rising ☐

  decreasing ☐

  staying at about the same level ☐

- Some scientists believe that the atmosphere is cooler now than in 1945 because of:

  dust ☐

  an increase in carbon dioxide ☐

  industry ☐

7. Is this statement correct or incorrect?

Radiation from the sun remains the same over the years. ☐

H. Understanding discourse

Listen to this lecturer giving you some exercises to work on before the next lecture. Note down the questions you are to answer.

_____

_____

_____

THE LANDSCAPE (1)

A. Understanding a printed text (1)

The following text will introduce you to the topic of the **landscape**. Look at the way it is divided into sections and paragraphs. Pay attention to the headings and notes in the margins.

Now look at these questions:

1. What two kinds of erosion are described?
2. What does weathering mean?

3. What kind of process is weathering?
4. What contributes most to erosion?
5. What are a stream's main functions in erosion?

Read the passage through and find the answers to the questions. Remember, you do not have to understand every word to answer them.

EROSION

1 All the processes by which rocks are worn down and by which the debris is carried away are included in the general term *erosion*. The underlying cause of erosion is gravity. Such agents of erosion as running water and glaciers derive their destructive abilities from gravity, and gravity is responsible for the transport of removed material to lower and lower elevations. The leveling of landscape by erosion is often referred to as *gradation*.

Erosion and gradation

Weathering

2 We have all seen the rough, pitted surfaces of old stone monuments and buildings and the progressive obliteration of their markings. This sort of disintegration, brought about by rainwater and atmospheric gases, is called *weathering*.

3 Weathering is in part a chemical process, in part a mechanical process. It participates in erosion in an important way by preparing rock material for easy removal by the more active erosional agents. Among the agents whose work is most obvious are streams, glaciers, wind, and waves. Less apparent is the erosional work of groundwater, water in crevices and channels beneath the surface. All these agents are capable of cutting slowly into solid, un-weathered rock, but their work is greatly speeded by the disintegration of rocks into the softer material of the weathered layer.

Weathering refers to the disintegration of rock surfaces in the open air

4 Some of the minerals in igneous and metamorphic rocks are especially susceptible to *chemical weathering*, since they were formed under conditions very different from those at the earth's surface and minerals stable under the former conditions are not necessarily stable under the latter. Most sedimentary rocks, on the other hand, consist of rock debris that has already undergone chemical weathering, and so are relatively resistant to further attack; the chief exception is limestone.

Chemical weathering

Mechanical weathering

Weathering and soil

Streams are the chief agent of erosion

5   Ferromagnesian minerals are readily attacked by atmospheric oxygen with the help of carbonic acid (formed by the solution of carbon dioxide in water) and of organic acids from decaying vegetation. Their iron content changes to rustlike compounds whose red and brown colors are familiar as stains on the surface of rocks containing these minerals. Feldspars and other silicates containing aluminum are in large part altered to clay minerals. Among common sedimentary rocks limestone is most readily attacked by chemical weathering because of the solubility of calcite in carbonic acid. Exposures of this rock can often be identified simply from the pitted surfaces and enlarged cracks that solution produces. Quartz and white mica are extremely resistant to chemical attack and usually remain as loose grains when the rest of a rock is thoroughly decayed. Rocks consisting wholly of silica, like chert and most quartzites, are practically immune to chemical weathering.

6   *Mechanical weathering* is often aided by chemical attack; not only is the structure of a rock weakened by the decomposition of its minerals, but fragments are actively wedged apart because the chemical changes in a mineral grain usually result in an increased volume. The most effective process of mechanical disintegration that does not involve chemical action is the freezing of water in crevices, since water expands when it turns into ice and considerable forces can be developed in this way. Just as water freezing in an automobile engine on a cold night may split the block, so water freezing in tiny cracks is an effective wedge for disrupting rocks. Plant roots aid in rock disintegration by growing and enlarging themselves in cracks.

7   Weathering processes clothe the naked rock of the earth's crust with a layer of debris made up largely of clay mixed with rock and mineral fragments. The upper part of the weathered layer, in which rock debris is mixed with decaying vegetable matter, is the soil. From a human point of view the formation of soil is by all odds the most important result of weathering.

Stream Erosion

8   By far the most important agent of erosion is the running water of streams. The work of glaciers, wind, and waves is impressive locally but, by comparison with running water, they play only minor roles in the shaping of the earth's landscapes. Even in deserts, mountain sides are carved with the unmistakable forms of stream-made valleys.

9   A stream performs two functions in erosion:

   1   Active cutting at the sides and bottom of its channel

   2   Transportation of debris supplied by weathering and by its own cutting

Its effectiveness in carrying debris depends on its slope and on the volume of water in flow. Its effectiveness in cutting a channel depends on these factors and also on the amount and kind of debris with which it is supplied. Sand grains, pebbles, and boulders are the tools that a stream uses to dig into its bed. Scraping them along its bottom and ramming them against its banks, a stream can cut its way through the hardest rocks; the rounded forms of stream channels in hard rock and the smoothly rounded surfaces of the pebbles in stream gravel are testimony to the effectiveness of this grinding and pounding mechanism.

10   An additional factor of prime importance in determining how rapidly a stream will erode its valley is the frequency of violent storms in its neighborhood. Often during a few hours of a heavy rain a stream accomplishes more than in months or years of normal flow. One reason that running water is the dominant erosional agent in deserts is that desert storms, when they do occur, are violent enough to send raging torrents down the normally dry valleys. Another reason is that there is little soil or vegetation to absorb water from a rainfall, so most of it remains on the surface to enhance the flash floods.

11   If we could watch the development of a river cutting downward through rock of uniform hardness, we would see repeated in slow motion the events that mark the growth of a gully cut in the soft material of a hillside. The gully is deepened, lengthened, and widened by the temporary stream formed during each successive rain. Deepening is accomplished by the downcutting of the stream. Lengthening takes place at the head of the gully, where the stream eats farther and farther into the hill. Widening is a direct result not so much of the stream's activity but of rainwash and slumping of material on the gully's sides. Thus the stream itself cuts like a blunt knife downward and backward into the hill, while secondary processes widen the gash. The combination of deepening and widening gives the gully its characteristic V-shaped cross section; the V is steep when downcutting is rapid compared with the work of rainwash and slumping, broader when downcutting is slow. As a gully grows older the rate of downcutting slackens, and the processes of widening make its cross section a broader and broader V.

The development of a gully in a hillside

Streams cut V-shaped channels

B. Check your understanding

Now read the text again carefully, looking up anything you do not understand. Then answer the following questions.

1. What is gradation?

2. What are the active erosional agents?

3. What is easily attacked by chemical weathering?

4. How are ferromagnesian minerals attacked?

5. What effect does chemical weathering have on feldspars?

6. What two examples of mechanical weathering agents are given?

7. What is an important result of weathering for mankind?

8. What is meant by a grinding and pounding mechanism?

9. What role do violent storms play in erosion by streams?

10. What are the three processes that lead to the development of a gully?

C. Increase your vocabulary

1. Look at paragraphs 1 and 2 again. Using your dictionary, complete the following table:

Noun	Verb	Adjective
erosion		
obliteration		
disintegration		
gravity		

2. Look at paragraphs 3 and 4 and say which words have the same meaning as:

- takes part in
- small cracks
- not likely to move or change
- scattered, broken pieces

3. Look at paragraph 5 again and explain the following words:

- decaying
- vegetation
- rustlike
- solubility
- exposure
- grain
- immune

4. Look at paragraph 6 again. Replace the words in *italics* with words taken from the paragraph:

I expect part of the old wall in my garden will *fall to pieces* in the end. There are a lot of *small cracks* in it, and water gets into them and freezes. There are also plants growing in the wall, and their roots must — I suppose —

be *getting bigger*. Both the ice and the plants seem to be *pushing* the stones apart. The stones themselves are clearly under some form of attack, because sometimes *small pieces* just drop off them.

5. Now look at paragraph 9 and explain the difference between these four words:

- scrape
- ram
- grind
- pound

6. Now look at paragraph 10 and say which words have the opposite meaning to:

- fails to achieve
- calm
- detract from

7. Now look at paragraph 11 and explain the following words:

- gully
- slumping
- rainwash
- slacken

D. Check your grammar

DESCRIBING

1. Shorten the following sentences without changing their meaning, like this:

Fog is a *cloud formation which lies at a low level*.
Fog is a *low-lying cloud formation*.

- A climate that changes.
- A temperature that varies.

- A river that moves slowly.
- A stream that flows fast.
- A surface that slopes outwards.
- Clouds that bear rain.

2. Shorten the following sentences without changing their meaning, like this:

Feldspar crystals have *points with ends that are blunt*.
Feldspar crystals have *blunt-pointed ends*.

- Silt which is blown by the wind accumulates in sheltered places.
- The silt then forms a claylike substance called loess which is buff in colour.
- Sand which is driven by the wind forms dunes.
- Dune sand is composed of grains that are rounded well.
- The sides of desert mountains are covered with the characteristic patterns of valleys that have been eroded by streams.

- A cirque looks like an amphitheatre with walls that are steep.
- The combination of deepening and widening gives a gully its characteristic cross-section which is shaped like a V.
- Crystals which have developed well make recognition of a mineral easy.
- We find rocks which have both coarse grains and fine grains on the earth's surface.
- An anticyclone is centred on a region which has a high pressure.

E. Understanding a lecture

Listen to this lecture on how an eroded landscape develops. Using the information the lecturer gives you, answer the questions below. The lecture is divided into sections. You should look at the illustrations on page 94 as you listen.

Section 1

Finish these statements correctly
- A stream or river first digs a

  gorge ☐

  cross-section ☐

  valley ☐

- The valley is

  U-shaped ☐

  V-shaped ☐

  S-shaped ☐

- At this stage of development a profile of the stream would show

  _____ and

  _____ and

  _____

Section 2

- When can a river not cut any further down?

  _____

  _____

- What happens when a river cannot cut any further down?

  _____

  _____

- What effects does this have?

  _____

Section 3

- When a stream's energy is no longer put into downcutting, where does it go?

  _____

  _____

- What is deposited on the flood plain?

  _____

- What is the difference between stage (d) and stage (e) in the diagram?

  _____

  _____

Section 4

- What term is given to a smaller stream that joins a larger one?

  _____

- How do tributaries develop?

_____

_____

- Note down the main characteristics of a fully developed system.

_____

_____

_____

_____

_____

_____

Section 5

- What three words does the lecturer use to describe landscapes at different stages in their development?

_____

_____

_____

Now write a summary of the lecture, using the information you have been given. The answers to the questions will help you.

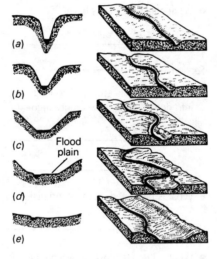

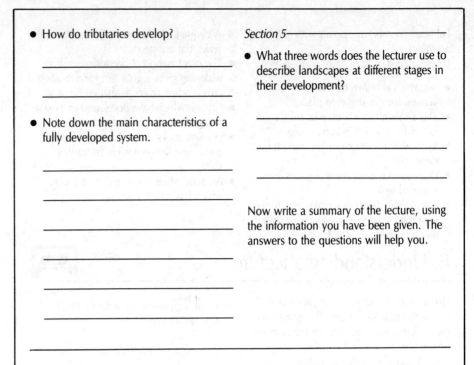

Figure 1. Successive stages in the development of a river valley. The general appearance of the valley at various times is shown at the right and the corresponding cross sections at the left.

(a)

(b)

(c) Flood plain

(d)

(e)

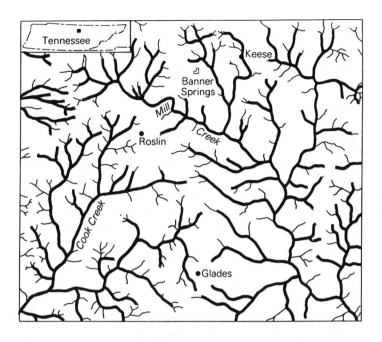

Figure 2. The typical treelike pattern of a fully developed drainage system.

Figure 3. The development of a landscape by stream erosion, from youth (*a*) through maturity (*b*) and old age (*c*).

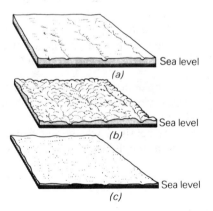

F. Understanding a printed text (2)

Read the following text carefully, looking up anything you do not understand.

Glaciers

1   In a cold climate with abundant snowfall, the snow of winter may not completely melt or evaporate during the following summer, and so a·deposit of snow accumulates from year to year. Partial melting and continual increase in pressure cause the lower part of a snow deposit to change gradually into ice. If the ice is sufficiently thick, gravity forces it to move slowly downhill. A moving mass of ice formed in this manner is called a *glacier*. Approximately 10 percent of the earth's land area is covered by glacial ice at the present time.

A glacier is a moving mass of ice

2   Today's glaciers are of two principal types:

1   *Valley glaciers*—found, for instance, in the Alps, on the Alaskan coast, in the western United States—are patches and tongues of dirty ice lying in mountain valleys. These glaciers move slowly down their valleys, melting copiously at their lower ends; the ‐combination of downward movement and melting keeps their ends in approximately the same position from year to year. Movement in the faster valley glaciers (a few feet per day) is sufficient to keep their lower ends well below timberline.

Valley glaciers

2   Glaciers of another type cover most of Greenland and Antarctica: huge masses of ice thousands of feet thick and thousands of square miles in area, engulfing hills as well as valleys, and appropriately called *continental glaciers* or *ice caps*. These, too, move downhill, but the "hill" is the slope of their upper surfaces. An ice cap has the shape of a broad dome, its surface sloping outward from a thick central portion of greatest snow accumulation: its motion is radially outward in all directions from its center. (Fig. 6.5). The icebergs of the polar seas are fragments that have broken off the edges of ice caps. Similar sheets of ice extended across Canada and northern Eurasia in relatively recent geological history.

Ice caps

3   Apparently a glacier moves by internal fracture and healing in the crystals of solid ice as well as by sliding along its bed. Like a stream, a glacier carries along rock fragments which serve as tools in cutting its bed. Some fragments are the debris of weathering that drop on the glacier from its sides; others are torn from its bed when melted water freezes in rock crevices. Fragments

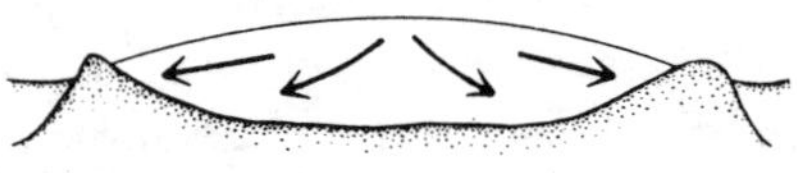

Fig. 6.5 Schematic cross section of an ice cap. The arrows show the direction of ice movement.

at the bottom surface of the glacier, held firmly in the grip of the ice and dragged slowly along its bed, gouge and polish the bedrock and are themselves flattened and scratched. Smoothed and striated rock surfaces and deposits of debris containing boulders with flattened sides are common near the ends of valley glaciers. Where such evidence of the grinding and polishing of ice erosion is found far from present-day glaciers, we have reason to infer that glaciation was present there in the past.

4   Valley glaciers form in valleys carved originally by streams. A mountain stream cuts like a knife vertically downward, letting slope wash, slumping, and minor tributaries shape its valley walls; by contrast, a glacier is a blunt erosional instrument which grinds down simultaneously all parts of its valley floor and far up the sides as well. Effects of this erosion are best seen in valleys that have been glaciated in the past but in which glaciers have dwindled greatly or disappeared. Typically such valleys have U-shaped cross sections with very steep sides, instead of the V shapes produced by stream erosion. Their heads are round, steep-walled amphitheaters called *cirques*, in contrast to the small gullies at the heads of stream valleys. Tributary streams often drop into a formerly glaciated valley over high cliffs because a large glacier carves out its channel much more actively than a small one does. A tributary valley left stranded high above its main valley is called a *hanging valley* and is often the scene of a spectacular waterfall.

Glacial erosion produces U-shaped valleys

Hanging valleys

5   Divides between cirques and between adjacent U-shaped valleys tend to be sharp ridges because of the steepness of the valley walls. In general, since valley glaciers produce deep gorges, steep slopes, and knifelike ridges, their effect is to make mountain topography extremely rugged. The earth's most spectacular mountain scenery is in regions (the Alps, the Rockies, the Himalayas) where valley glaciers were large and numerous several thousand years ago.

6   The influence of ice caps on landscapes is very different from that of valley glaciers. We cannot, of course, observe directly the effect of existing ice caps on the buried landscapes of Greenland and Antarctica, but larger ice caps that once covered much of Northern Europe and North America have left clear records of their erosional activity, which we can easily see from the rounded hills and valleys, the abundant lakes and swamps so characteristic of these regions. Like a gigantic piece of sandpaper, an ice cap rounds off sharp corners, wears down hills, and fills depressions with debris, leaving innumerable shallow basins which form lakes when the ice recedes.
innumerable shallow basins which form lakes when the ice recedes.

Northern Europe and North America were once covered by ice caps

7   Glacial erosion is locally very impressive, particularly in high mountains. The amount of debris and the size of the boulders that a glacier can carry are often startling. But in general, on a worldwide basis, the erosional work accomplished by glaciers is small. Only rarely have they eroded rock surfaces deeply, and the amount of material transported long distances is insignificant compared with that carried by streams. Most glaciers of today are but feeble descendants of mighty ancestors, but even these ancestors succeeded only in modifying landscapes already shaped by running water.

On a worldwide basis, glacial erosion is minor

G. Check your understanding

1. Look at the first paragraph and say whether these statements are correct or incorrect:

- A glacier is created by unmelted snow. ☐
- Gravity is the force that moves the glacier. ☐

2. Look at paragraph 2 again. Can you describe the main differences between a valley glacier and a continental glacier?

3. Look at paragraph 3 and say which words have the same meaning as:

- break/breaking
- striped/furrowed
- conclude/reach an opinion

4. Look at paragraph 3 again. In that paragraph you have the following words. Write sentences showing you understand their meanings:

- drag
- gouge
- polish
- flatten
- scratch
- striated

5. Look at paragraph 4 and say which words have the opposite meaning to:

- sharp
- at different times
- increased

6. Now look at paragraphs 5–7 and say which words have the same meaning as:

- very sharp
- enormous
- under the ground
- rough/uneven/rocky
- very surprising
- weak

H. Understanding discourse

A lecturer is again going to give you questions which you must work on. This time he is going to give you three. Note down the questions.

_____

_____

_____

THE LANDSCAPE (2)

A. Understanding a printed text (1)

The following text continues the topic of the **landscape**. Look at the way it is divided into sections and paragraphs. Pay attention to the headings and notes in the margins, and to the illustration and caption.

Now look at these questions:

1. What is this text about?
2. What three important characteristics of sediments does the writer refer to?

3. What is the third section about?
4. What are the two types of glacial deposits referred to?

Read the passage through and find the answers to the questions. Remember, you do not have to understand every word to answer them.

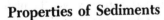

SEDIMENTATION

1 Most of the material transported by the agents of erosion is eventually deposited to form *sediments* of various sorts. Only substances in solution can escape such deposition; ions of various salts carried by streams to lakes and oceans may remain dissolved indefinitely. The salt of the ocean is chiefly an accumulation of material dissolved out of rocks by seawater itself, rain, rivers, and groundwater. Under some conditions part of the dissolved material may form sediments; salts like calcium carbonate precipitate readily, and others appear when evaporation concentrates the water of a salt lake or an arm of the sea.

Properties of Sediments

2   The ultimate destination of erosional debris is the ocean, and the most widespread sediments accumulate in shallow parts of the ocean near continental margins. But much sedimentary material is carried to the sea in stages, deposited first in thick layers elsewhere—in lakes, in desert basins, in stream valleys. Each of the various erosional agents has its own characteristic ways of depositing its load, and these ways leave their stamp on the character of the deposits formed. Since sediments laid down ages ago often retain many of their original characteristics, an acquaintance with the processes of deposition enables us to infer the probable origin of older deposits. In this way we can reconstruct past conditions of erosion and sedimentation and so gain insight into many chapters of earth history.

The largest deposits of sediments occur near continental margins

3   An important characteristic of sedimentary deposits is their degree of *sorting*, which refers to the extent of separation of fine material from coarse—whether boulders, pebbles, sand, and clay are mixed together or are segregated in different layers. Another feature that may help to identify a sediment's origin is the kind of *bedding* it shows. Slight changes in the composition or grain size of a sediment produce layers of different appearance, which may lie parallel to one another or at different angles. The latter situation, called *cross-bedding*, can arise from turbulent flow which produces patterns of ripples on the channel bottom; when the angles between the beds are steep and each bed is more than about a foot thick, the deposits are more likely to have been laid down by winds in the form of dunes than by streams. Some sediments have practically no layering, but retain the same color and texture through great thicknesses; in others each bed or *stratum* is sharply marked off from those above and below by differences in color and grain size. The layers of stratified deposits are sometimes uniform and parallel over long distances and sometimes show abrupt variations in thickness.

Stream Deposits

4   Streams, the chief agents of erosion, lose some of the debris they carry whenever their speeds drop or their volumes of water decrease. Four sites of deposition are common:

1   Debris carried in time of flood is deposited in gravel banks and sandbars on the stream bed when the swiftly flowing waters begin to recede.

2   The flood plain of a meandering river is a site of deposition whenever the river overflows its banks and loses speed as it spreads over the plain. In Egypt, for example, before construction of the Aswan Dam, the fertility of the soil was maintained for centuries by the deposit of black silt left each year when the Nile was in flood.

3   A common site of deposition is the point where a stream emerges from a steep mountain valley and slows down as it flows onto a plain. Such a deposit, usually taking the form of a low cone pointing upstream, is called an *alluvial fan*.

4   A similar deposit is formed when a stream's flow is stopped abruptly as it flows into a lake or sea. This kind of deposit, built largely under water and with a surface usually much flatter than that of an alluvial fan, is called a *delta*.

5   Streams can transport fragments of all sizes, from fine clay particles to large boulders. A smoothly flowing stream tends to deposit the coarse fragments it carries first, with finer and finer particles settling out farther and farther along its path. Thus a well-sorted sediment, which consists of particles of very nearly the same size, indicates that such a stream was responsible. On the other hand, a turbulent stream is only fair as a sorting agent, so that individual layers in its deposits usually contain mixtures of sand and gravel or of sand and clay. Pebbles and boulders, angular when they start out, become rounded when a stream has rolled them along its channel. The constant shifting of stream courses, the filling of old channels and cutting of new ones, and the building and tearing down of gravel banks and sandbars lead to conspicuously uneven bedding. This irregular bedding—thin layers of gravel, sand, and silt which thicken or pinch out abruptly, often cross-bedded—is the outstanding characteristic of stream deposits.

6   Fragments carried by a swift stream are subjected to continual hammering against one another and against the stream bed, and are constantly exposed to the agents of weathering. In such an environment only the toughest and most resistant minerals can survive. Stream gravels that have not traveled far from their source may contain pebbles of many different rock types, but gravels that a stream has carried for long distances contain hard rocks almost exclusively. Since quartz is the hardest and most resistant of common minerals, material that has been battered down to sand-grain size usually contains an abundance of quartz. Fine material in stream sediments consists chiefly of clay minerals.

Stream gravels

Glacial Deposits

7   Some of the material scraped from its channel by a glacier is heaped up at its lower end where the ice melts and some is spread as a layer of irregular thickness beneath the ice. The pile of debris around the end of the glacier, called a *moraine,* is left as a low ridge of hummocky topography when the glacier melts back. Moraines in mountain valleys and in the North Central states are part of the evidence for a former wide extent of glaciation.

8   The material deposited directly by ice is called *till,* and is a characteristic indiscriminate mixture of fine and coarse material. Huge boulders are often embedded in the abundant, fine, claylike material that a glacier produces by its polishing action. Most of the boulders are angular; a few are rounded and show flattened, scratched faces produced as they were dragged along the bed of the glacier.

Till is the material deposited by a glacier

B. Check your understanding

Now read the text again carefully, looking up anything you do not understand. Then answer the following questions.

1. What is a sediment?

2. Where does all debris end up?

3. How is sedimentary material carried to the sea?

4. Why does knowing the processes of deposition help us?

5. Can you explain *sorting. bedding* and *cross-bedding*?

6. What is a *stratum*?

7. When a stream is in flood, where does the debris go?

8. Where do *alluvial fans* occur?

9. What is the outstanding characteristic of stream deposits?

10. Can you explain the terms *moraine* and *till*?

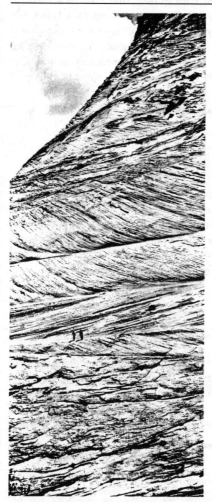

The action of winds is probably responsible for this striking example of cross-bedding in Utah.

C. Increase your vocabulary

1. Look at the first paragraph and say which words are used to mean:

- for an unlimited length of time
- a gathering together

2. Now look at paragraph 2 again and say which words have the opposite meaning to:

- rare
- in other places

3. Now look at paragraph 3 and say which words have the same meaning as:

- sudden
- small
- rough
- violently disturbed
- almost
- the arrangement of the parts that make up something
- arranged in strata

4. Now look at paragraph 5 and say which words have the same meaning as

- small pieces
- shows, points to
- easily seen
- attracting notice

5. Now look at paragraph 6. In it the two words *constant* and *continual* are used.

Is there any difference between them and the word *continuous*?

6. Now look at paragraphs 7 and 8 and say which words match these definitions:

- like small hills
- description of the surface features of a place or district
- without any particular order
- fixed firmly

7. Using your dictionary, complete the following table.

Noun	Adjective	Verb
		recede
fertility		
		emerge
	resistant	
		indicate
extent		

D. Check your grammar

PARAGRAPH WRITING

Make complete sentences out of the following notes, putting the verbs in brackets in the right tense. Then arrange the sentences into two paragraphs. Make sure that the sentences follow each other logically and that each paragraph makes sense. Start with the heading:

UNDERSEA CURRENTS

- sandbars/beaches/visible/of/and/deposits/and/waves/currents

  (*include*)

- rivers/gravel/and/outward/by/clay/sand

  (*carry*)

  _____

- most/agents/the/currents/the/of/of/deposition/sea/important/the/of

  (*be*)

  _____

- also/the/shore/rip currents/they/directly/from/by

  (*carry*)

  _____

- by/of/sediment/because/this/far/the/amount/largest/they

  (*be; handle*)

  _____

- strong/seaward/rip current/current/a/a/but/narrow

  (*be*)

  _____

- whenever/the/weak/too/them/materials/these/to carry/current

  (*drop; become*)

  _____

- materials/coastlines/eroded/from/action/by/currents/wave/the

  (*deposit*)

  _____

- sea/in/deposition/ways/the/beneath/several

  (*take place*)

  _____

- places/creatures/an/deposited/dead/material/in/of/marine/the/some/of/shells/part/the/important

  (*be*)

  _____

- the/breaking/midst/of/rip currents/waves/in

  (*find*)

  _____

- brought/streams/also/winds/and/the/they/glaciers/ocean/the/by/to/debris

  (*deposit*)

  _____

- sediments/however/underwater/most

  (*lay down*)

  _____

- chemical/notably/saturated/calcium carbonate/as/some/when/locally/seawater/salts/precipitates

  (*deposit; become*)

  _____

E. Understanding a lecture

Listen to this lecture on waves and currents.
Using the information the lecturer gives you,
answer the questions below. The lecture is
divided into sections.

Section 1—————————————

- What is the lecturer going to talk about?

  _____

- The lecturer refers to:

  one kind of current ☐

  two kinds of current ☐

  three kinds of current ☐

  four kinds of current ☐

- Write a short note for yourself on

  A rip current_____

  _____

  A longshore current_____

  _____

- What two factors are responsible for the shape of a coastline?

  _____

  _____

- For earth scientists, the most important effect of wave activity is:

  the creation of beautiful coastlines ☐

  the creation of debris ☐

  the removal of debris to other places ☐

  the activity itself ☐

Section 2——————————

- Is this statement correct or incorrect?

  Waves on a lakeshore and waves on a coastline have the same range. ☐

- In what way do waves act on the land?

  _____

  _____

Section 3——————————

- Label Figure 1, showing as much of the information that the lecturer gives you as you can. Remember to say what the diagram is.

Section 4——————————

- Label Figure 2, showing as much of the information that the lecturer gives you as you can. Remember to say what the diagram is.

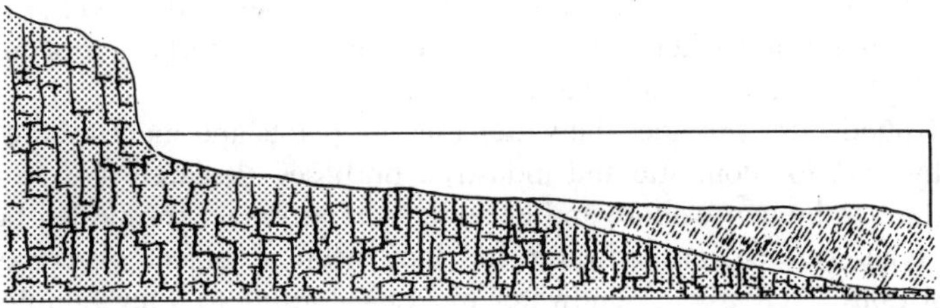

Fig. 1

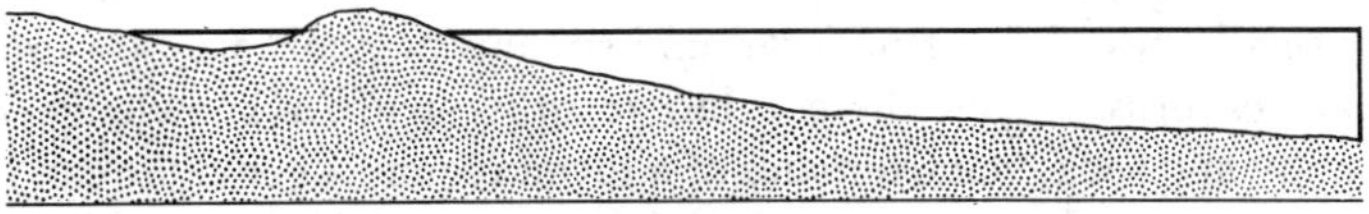

Fig. 2

F. Understanding a printed text (2)

Read the following text carefully, looking up anything you do not understand.

GROUNDWATER

1 Much of the water that falls as rain does not run off immediately in streams but soaks into the ground. All water that thus penetrates the surface is called *groundwater*.

2   The soil, the weathered layer, and any porous rocks beneath act together as a huge sponge, absorbing great quantities of water into their interstices. During and immediately after a heavy rain all empty spaces in the sponge may be filled, and the ground is then said to be *saturated* with water. When the rain has stopped, water slowly drains away from hills into the adjacent valleys. A few days after a rain porous material in the upper part of a hill contains relatively little moisture, while that in the lower part may still be saturated. Another rainfall would raise the upper level of the saturated zone; a prolonged drought would lower it. The fluctuating upper surface of the saturated zone is called the *water table*.

Movement of Groundwater

3   Beneath valleys the water table is ordinarily nearer the surface than under adjacent hills, since water from the saturated zone continually moves outward into valleys. These general relations are shown in Fig. 6.8. Movement of groundwater in the saturated zone is principally a slow seeping downward and sideward into streams, lakes, and swamps. The motion is rapid through coarse material like sand or gravel, very slow through fine material like clay. It is this flow of groundwater that maintains streams when rain is not falling; a stream goes dry only when the water table drops below the level of its bed. A *spring* is formed where groundwater comes to the surface in a more or less definite channel, usually on a hillside.

4   Groundwater provides the water used by plants and much of the water used by man for domestic and industrial purposes. Because it is so vitally important to human welfare and because its movements are hidden beneath the ground surface, groundwater has long been a subject of extravagant superstitions. Actually, groundwater moves according to a few simple rules: its source is rain; it moves in a general downward direction; its motion consists of a slow seepage, faster in sand or gravel than in clay, faster in large cracks than in small ones; definite underground streams or pools are rare except in limestone caverns. From these rules, together with a knowledge of the topography and rock characteristics of a given region, a geologist can usually make accurate predictions as to the whereabouts and motions of available groundwater.

5   Although groundwater movement is slow, its erosional activity is by no means negligible. It can accomplish little mechanical wear, but its intimate contact with rocks and soil enables it to dissolve much soluble material. The dissolved substances are in part transported to neighboring streams, in part redeposited at other points in the weathered layer or bedrock. Dissolved material is responsible for the *hardness* of water from many wells.

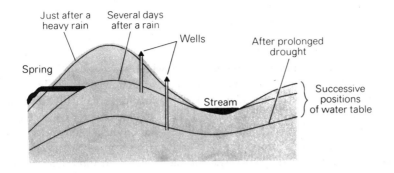

Fig. 6.8 Schematic cross section through a landscape underlain by porous material. The position of the water table is shown just after a heavy rain, several days later, and after a prolonged drought. The spring and upper well would be dry during the drought.

6   In regions underlaid by limestone, most easily soluble of ordinary rocks, the solvent action of groundwater makes itself conspicuous by the formation of caverns. A cavern is produced when water moving through tiny cracks in limestone gradually enlarges the cracks by dissolving and removing adjacent rock material. The roof of a cavern near the surface may collapse to form a *sinkhole*. A distinctive *karst topography* occurs in places where underground channels, caverns, and sinkholes are abundant. The name comes from the Karst region of Yugoslavia, where such features are especially common.

Karst topography

7   The activity of groundwater may extend downward for some hundreds or thousands of feet, the depth in a given region depending on the kinds of rock present. Nearly all rocks within a short distance of the surface have sufficient pore space or are sufficiently cracked to permit some circulation, although in massive igneous and metamorphic rocks the amount of groundwater may be very small. At lower levels cracks become too small and too scarce to permit free movement. Thus deep mines often have plenty of water in their upper parts but so little lower down that dust from drilling and blasting becomes a problem.

Groundwater is present only in the upper part of the crust

Hard Water

8   Hard water contains dissolved minerals which prevent soap from forming suds, react with soap to produce a precipitate, and form insoluble deposits in boilers and teakettles. Calcium and magnesium ions are usually responsible for hard water. These ions are often present in groundwater because of the solvent action of water containing dissolved carbon dioxide on rocks such as limestone. To "soften" water, the Ca^{2+} and Mg^{2+} ions must be removed, which can be done in a variety of ways. In one common method, hard water is passed through a zeolite column; zeolite is a mineral which absorbs Ca^{2+} and Mg^{2+} ions into its structure while releasing an equivalent number of Na$^+$ (sodium) ions. Since Na$^+$ ions do not affect soap, nor do sodium compounds precipitate out from hot water, the water is now soft.

Deposition by Groundwater

Veins consist of minerals
deposited from solution

9   Deposition by groundwater is almost entirely chemical precipitation from solution. The precipitation may be brought about by evaporation of the water, by mixing of groundwater from different sources, by a lowering of temperature, or by the escape of a gas when pressure is reduced. One of the most important geologic activities of groundwater is the depositing of material in the pore spaces of sediments, which helps to convert the sediments into rock. Much dissolved material is deposited along open cracks to form *veins,* common in all kinds of rocks. The usual vein minerals are quartz and calcite, but some veins contain commercially valuable minerals. More spectacular examples of groundwater deposition are the *stalactites* that hang from the roofs of limestone caverns and the colorful deposits often found around hot springs and geysers.

G. Check your understanding

1. Look at paragraphs 1 and 2 and complete the following:

• Ground water is

water that stays on the surface. ☐

water that runs away in streams. ☐

water that sinks below the surface. ☐

water that falls as rain. ☐

• Is this statement correct or incorrect?

The water table is always close to the earth's surface. ☐

2. Now look at paragraph 3 again. Are these statements correct or incorrect?

• Water from below the water table can only move downwards. ☐

• The speed of movement of water depends on the material it moves through. ☐

• A stream dries up when there is no more groundwater in the surrounding hills. ☐

3. Now look at paragraph 4 again and complete the following:

• For humanity, groundwater is

very important. ☐

insignificant. ☐

of some importance. ☐

of no importance at all. ☐

Is this statement correct or incorrect?

- Groundwater moves according to very complicated rules. ☐

4. Now look at paragraph 5 again. Are these statements correct or incorrect?

- Groundwater does not cause erosion of any kind. ☐

- The hardness of water is decided by the amount of groundwater. ☐

5. Now look at paragraph 6 again. Are these statements correct or incorrect?

- Limestone is the rock groundwater dissolves most easily. ☐

- A sinkhole is a kind of underground waterfall. ☐

6. Now look at paragraph 7 again. Are these statements correct or incorrect?

- There are two kinds of rock in which the quantity of groundwater may not be very great. ☐

- In some mines, there may be more water near the surface than near the bottom. ☐

7. Now look at paragraph 8 again. Is this statement correct or incorrect?

- To convert hard water into soft two kinds of ion must be removed. ☐

8. Now look at paragraph 9 again. Can you explain the terms

- vein
- stalactite

H. Understanding discourse

Listen to the lecturer talking about **lithification**. Below you can see the notes a student has made on what the lecturer is saying. Decide whether the student's notes are correct or incorrect.

Lithification is the process that takes place when sediments harden into rocks.

Lithification is a simple process.

Lithification takes place within 1000 years of starting.

There is only one change: compaction.

Compaction is when grains are squeezed together.

Compaction is caused by the pressure of deposits above the sediments.

During compaction, calcite crystals in limy deposits grow larger, but they do not interlock.

The following short test is for you to check whether you are learning the skills you will need to study Earth Sciences in English. It is for *your* information. It is *not* an examination. You may use a dictionary.

A. Reading

Read the following text and then answer the questions.

VULCANISM

A volcano is an opening through which molten rock emerges

A volcano is an opening in the earth's crust through which molten rock, usually called *magma* while underground and *lava* aboveground, pours forth. Because the emerging material accumulates near the orifice, most volcanoes in the course of time build up mountains with a characteristic conical shape that steepens toward the top, with a small depression or crater at the summit. Lava escapes almost continuously from a few volcanoes, but the majority are active only at intervals.

Volcanic Eruptions

A volcanic eruption is one of the most awesome spectacles in all nature. Usually earthquakes provide a warning a few hours or a few days beforehand—minor shocks probably caused by the movement of gases and liquids underground. An explosion or a series of explosions begins the eruption, sending a great cloud billowing upward from the crater. In the cloud are various gases, dust, fragments of solid material blown from the crater and the upper part of the volcano's orifice, and larger solid fragments representing molten rock blown to bits and hurled upward by the violence of the explosions.

Gas continues to issue in great quantities, and explosions recur at intervals. The cloud may persist for days or weeks with its lower part glowing red at night. Activity gradually slackens, and presently a tongue of white-hot lava spills over the edge of the crater or pours out of a fissure on the mountain slope. Other flows may follow the first, and explosive activity may continue with diminished intensity. Slowly the volcano becomes quiescent, until only a small steam cloud above the crater suggests its activity.

Not all eruptions by any means follow this particular pattern. Volcanoes are notoriously individualistic, each one having some quirks of behavior not shared by others. In one group of volcanoes the explosive type of activity is dominant, little or no fluid lava appearing during eruptions. Cones of these volcanoes, built entirely of fragmental material ejected in a solid or nearly solid state, are very steep sided; examples are found in the West Indies, in Japan, and in the Philippines. Other volcanoes, like those of Hawaii, have eruptions characterized by quiet lava flows with little explosive activity. Mountains built by these volcanoes are broad and gently sloping, quite different from the usual volcanic structure. The most common kind of volcano is neither wholly of the "explosive" type nor wholly of the "quiet" type, but has eruptions in which both lava flows and gas explosions occur.

The chief factors that determine whether an eruption will tend to be a largely quiet lava flow or tend to be explosive are the viscosity of the magma and the amount of gas it contains. (The greater the viscosity of a liquid, the less freely it flows: honey is more viscous than water.) Magma is a complex mixture of the oxides of various metals with silica and usually has an abundance of gas dissolved in it under pressure. Like most molten silicates it is extremely viscous, and with rare exceptions lava creeps downhill slowly, like thick syrup or tar. The viscosity depends upon chemical composition; magmas with high percentages of silica are the most viscous. The presence of gas also affects viscosity; magmas with little gas are the most viscous. If the magma feeding a volcano happens to be rich in both gas and silica, the eruption will be explosive. A magma with modest gas and silica contents results in a quiet eruption.

The gaseous products of volcanic activity include water vapor, carbon dioxide, nitrogen, hydrogen, and various sulfur compounds. The most prominent constituent is water vapor. Some of it comes from groundwater heated by magma, some comes from the combination of hydrogen in the magma with atmospheric oxygen, and some was formerly incorporated in rocks deep in the crust and is carried upward by the magma to be released at the surface. Much of the water vapor condenses when it escapes to give rise to the torrential rains that often accompany eruptions.

Explosive volcanoes emit solid material that forms steep cones

Quiet volcanoes emit lava that solidifies into gently sloping mountains

The properties of the magma (underground molten rock) involved determine the nature of a volcanic eruption

Answer these questions:

1. Is this statement correct or incorrect?

● Magma and lava are both terms used to describe molten rock. ☐

2. Choose the correct completion of the following statement:

● The first warning of volcanic eruption is usually given by

   the movement of gases and liquids. ☐

   minor shocks in the earth. ☐

   a great cloud. ☐

   one or more explosions. ☐

3. Say whether the following statements are correct or incorrect:

- The writer lists four components of the cloud issuing from a crater. ☐
- Lava is only spilled out from the crater of a volcano. ☐
- The greatest explosions occur when lava is spilled out. ☐

4. Choose the correct completion of the following statement:

- Individual volcanoes

  usually follow the same pattern as all other volcanoes. ☐

  follow their own pattern. ☐

  do not share any characteristics with other volcanoes. ☐

  always follow the same pattern as others in their group. ☐

5. Say whether the following statements are correct or incorrect:

- Volcanoes with gently-sloping sides can be found in the Philippines. ☐
- The more viscous the lava, the faster it flows. ☐
- Quiet eruptions are due to the presence of a large amount of gas. ☐
- Water vapour is a minor product of volcanic eruptions. ☐

B. Writing

Read the following text. Then, using your own words, explain the reasons why granite is believed to have hardened from the molten state.

Intrusive rocks have coarser grains than volcanic rocks because their slower cooling has permitted larger mineral crystals to form

Intrusive Rocks

Molten rock that rises through the earth's crust but does not reach the surface solidifies to form intrusive bodies (often called *plutons*) of various kinds. Because cooling in these bodies is slower than at the surface, intrusive igneous rocks are in general coarser-grained than volcanic rocks. We find such coarse-grained rocks exposed at the surface only when deep erosion has uncovered them after their solidification.

The igneous origin of volcanic rocks is clear enough, for we can actually watch lava harden to solid rock. But no one has ever seen an intrusive rock like granite in a liquid state in nature. The belief that granite was once molten follows from indirect evidence such as the following:

Why granite is believed to have hardened from a molten state

1 Granite shows the same relations among its minerals that a volcanic rock shows under the microscope: The separate grains are intergrown, and those with higher melting points show by their better crystal forms that they crystallized a little earlier.

2 In some small intrusive formations every gradation can be found between coarse granite and a rock indistinguishable from the volcanic rock rhyolite, whose igneous origin is established by direct observation.

3 Granite is found in masses that cut across layers of sedimentary rock and from which small irregular branches and stringers penetrate into the surrounding rocks; sometimes blocks of the sedimentary rocks are found completely engulfed by the granite.

4 That granite was at a high enough temperature to be molten is shown by the baking and recrystallization of the rocks that it intrudes.

It should be mentioned that not all granite bodies were formed from magmas that flowed from one place to another; some came into being as a result of the melting (or, perhaps, recrystallization without actual melting) of other rocks without any change in location having taken place.

C. Listening

You will now hear part of a lecture. Listen to each section of the lecture twice. After you have listened to each section for the second time, answer the questions below. Here is the lecture.

Section 1

1. What is the lecturer going to talk about?

_____

2. What does that mean?

_____

Section 2

3. What is the first kind of movement?

_____

Section 3

4. What is the second kind of movement?

_____

Section 4

5. What is the third kind of movement?

_____

Section 5

6. What does Diagram 1 illustrate?

_____

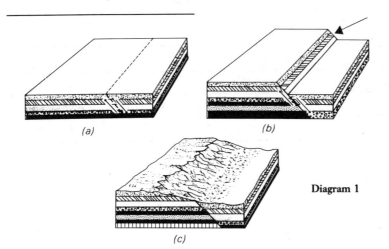

(a)

(b)

(c)

Diagram 1

7. Note down what (a) illustrates

_____

_____

8. Note down what (b) illustrates

_____

_____

9. What does the arrow point to?

_____

10. Note down what (c) illustrates

_____

_____

11. What is the cause of this kind of fault?

_____

12. What is the result?

_____

Section 6————————————————

Make notes on the following points the
lecturer covers.

13. Type of fault _____

14. Description _____

15. Cause _____

16. Result _____

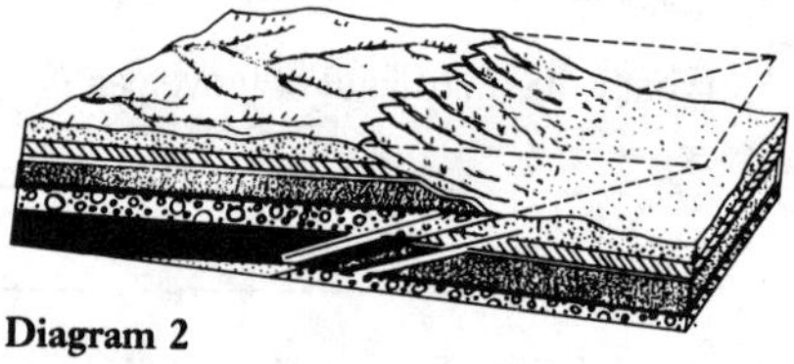

Diagram 2

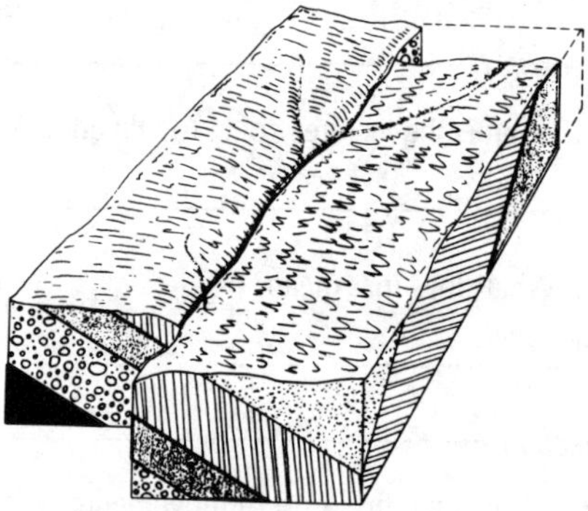

Diagram 3

Section 7————————————————

17. Type of fault _____

18. Description _____

19. Cause _____

20. Result _____

INSIDE THE EARTH

A. Understanding a printed text (1)

The following text will introduce you to the topic of **earthquakes**. Look at the way it is divided into sections and paragraphs. Pay attention to the headings and notes in the margins, and to the illustrations and captions.

Now look at these questions:

1. What does the writer describe in the first paragraph?

2. What does Fig. 8.1 illustrate?
3. What instruments are used to detect vibrations due to earthquakes?
4. What is the Richter scale?
5. What is the last paragraph about?

Read the passage through to find the answers to the questions. Remember, you do not have to understand every word to answer them.

EARTHQUAKE WAVES

1 An earthquake, the most destructive of natural phenomena, consists of rapid vibratory motions of rock near the earth's surface. A single shock usually lasts no more than a few seconds, though severe quakes may last for as much as three min; even in such brief times the damage done may be immense. The rapidity of the vibrations rather than the actual displacements involved is responsible for the damage. Man-made structures are shaken to pieces if they are too rigid to follow the back-and-forth motions of the underlying rock, and landslides are common. Widespread fires frequently follow earthquakes in inhabited regions since broken water mains hinder their control. But there is one useful feature of earthquakes: By studying the waves they send out, it is possible to infer a surprising amount about the nature of the earth's interior.

Earthquakes

2 Earthquakes occur without warning. Usually the first shock is the most severe, with disturbances of lessening intensity following at intervals for days or months afterward. A major earthquake may be felt over many thousands of square kilometers, but its destructiveness is limited to a much smaller area.

3 The great majority of earthquakes are caused by the sudden displacement of crustal blocks along faults. A fault, as we learned in the previous chapter, is the scar left by a fracture which occurred when the stresses developed within the crust became too great for the rock to support. Additional stress may accumulate to the point where further slippage takes place, and this slippage in turn sends out the shock waves that are characteristic of an earthquake. The event responsible for an earthquake typically involves an area within the crust some tens of kilometers across located within a few kilometers of the surface, but in a fair number of cases depths of up to several hundred kilometers below the crust have been established. The place where an earthquake originates is called its *focus*, and its *epicenter* is the point on the earth's surface directly above the focus (Fig. 8.1).

Most earthquakes are due to rock movement along faults

Focus and epicenter

4   Sensitive instruments called *seismographs* have been devised which respond to the vibrations of even distant earthquakes. Seismographs of different types are needed to respond to vertical and horizontal movements, as shown in Figs. 8.2 and 8.3. A vertical seismograph and two horizontal ones, one for the north-south direction and the other for the east-west direction, are needed at each observatory. Several hundred seismological stations are in operation around the world, and the data they obtain are routinely compared and correlated. It is possible to establish from such data where the focus of a given earthquake is located and something about how much energy it has released.

5   Earthquake severity is usually expressed on the *Richter scale,* which is based upon the maximum amplitude of an earthquake's vibrations. Each step of 1 on this scale represents a change in vibrational amplitude of a factor of 10 and a change in energy release of a factor of about 30; thus an earthquake of magnitude 5 produces vibrations 10 times larger than one of magnitude 4 and evolves 30 times more energy. An earthquake of magnitude 0 is barely capable of being detected, and the energy released, if it could be concentrated, is just about sufficient to blow up a tree stump. An inhabited area will suffer some damage if a magnitude 4.5 quake occurs nearby, and one of magnitude 6 or more may lead to significant destruction. The energy associated with a magnitude 6 earthquake is equivalent to that of a medium-size nuclear bomb, though its effects are different because the earthquake energy is spread out over a much wider area. The energy released in a magnitude 8.6 earthquake, the greatest that have occurred to date, is about double the energy content of the coal and oil produced each year in the entire world; the Alaska earthquake of 1964 was of nearly this magnitude.

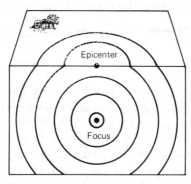

Fig. 8.1 The vibrations of an earthquake spread out from its focus; the epicenter is the place on the earth's surface directly above the focus.

6   Of the million or so earthquakes per year strong enough to be experienced as such (that is, of magnitude 2.5 or more), only a small proportion liberate enough energy to do serious damage to man-made structures. About 15 really violent earthquakes (magnitude 7 or more) occur each year on the average, and only 9 of magnitude 8.4 to 8.6 have occurred since 1899. Regions in which severe earthquakes are comparatively frequent include the mountain chains that fringe the Pacific and a broad belt extending from the Mediterranean basin across southern Asia to China. Major earthquakes have occurred sporadically elsewhere, but by far the greatest number have been concentrated in these zones. In or near the earthquake belts lie most of the world's active volcanoes (see Fig. 7.2)—which, as we shall see in Chap. 10, is no coincidence.

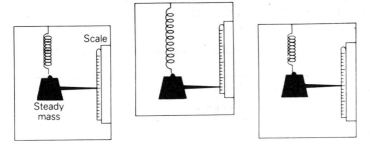

Fig. 8.2 The principle of the vertical seismograph. The suspended mass has a very long period of oscillation, and hence it remains very nearly stationary in space as the box and scale move up and down when earthquake waves arrive. Only vertical movements of the earth's surface are recorded by this instrument.

Fig. 8.3 A horizontal pendulum seismograph. This instrument responds to horizontal movements of the earth's surface.

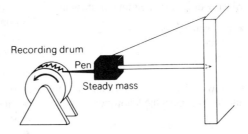

B. Check your understanding

Now read the text again carefully, looking up anything you do not understand. Then answer the following questions.

1. What does an earthquake consist of?

2. How long does a shock last?

3. What use are earthquakes?

4. What are most earthquakes caused by?

5. What do the terms *focus* and *epicentre* mean?

6. Why do we need different kinds of seismograph?

7. What can we establish from the data collected by seismological stations?

8. What does each step on the Richter scale show?

9. What are the strongest earthquakes so far recorded?

10. How rare are serious earthquakes?

C. Increase your vocabulary

1. Now look at the first paragraph again. Using your dictionary, complete the following table:

Noun	Adjective	Verb
	destructive	
	vibratory	
damage		
structure		

2. Look at the first paragraph again and try to explain the following:

- back-and-forth
- landslide
- water mains

3. Now look at paragraphs 2 and 3 and say which words have the same meaning as:

- as a general rule
- situated
- quite a lot

4. Now look at paragraphs 2 and 3 again and try to explain the following:

- square kilometer
- the difference between *destruction* and *destructiveness*
- stress
- crust

5. Now look at paragraph 4 and say what words could replace the following:

- as a matter of course
- information
- set free
- get
- far away

6. Now look at paragraph 5 again and try to explain the following:

- amplitude
- magnitude
- evolves
- factor of 10

7. Now look at paragraph 6. Can you produce sentences that show you know the meaning of the following words as used in this text?

- man-made
- severe
- fringe
- sporadic
- zone
- belt

D. Check your grammar

1. Which of the following adjectives can you make the opposite of using the prefixes in-, un-, ir- or dis-?

- responsible
- frequent
- broken
- surprising
- interior
- major

- additional
- characteristic
- direct
- proportionate
- vertical
- large
- capable
- wide
- active

2. Look at the map of the world below. It shows the principal earthquake and volcanic regions of the world. The principal earthquake areas are shown in tints and the principal volcanic regions are shown in black. Make statements about different areas of the world, like this:

Earthquakes are not to be expected in the Sahara.
Volcanic eruptions are to be anticipated in . . .

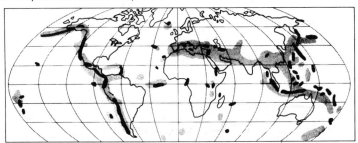

> **Do you remember?**
> Earthquakes *are* (not) *to be* expected in . . .

E. Understanding a lecture

Listen to this lecture on earthquake waves. Using the information the lecturer gives you, answer the questions below. The lecture is divided into sections:

Section 1

- What is the subject of the lecture?

- How many kinds of wave are there?

Section 2

- What kind of wave is the lecturer talking about in this section?

- Label the diagram on the dotted lines:

Diagram 1

Section 3

- What kind of wave is the lecturer talking about in this section?

  _____

- How do the individual particles of string move?

  _____

- How does the lecturer describe the difference between these two kinds of wave?

  _____

Diagram 2

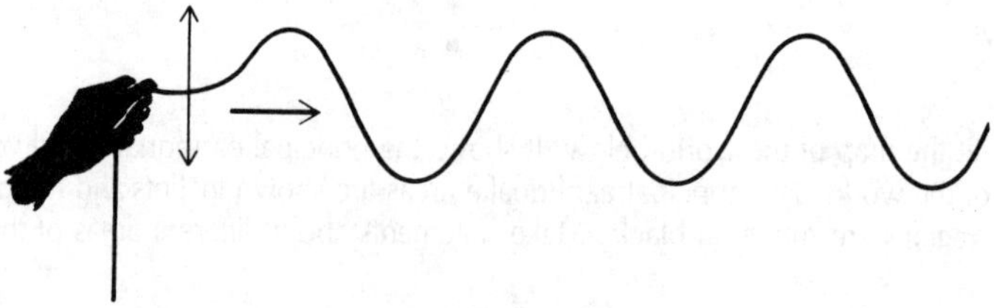

Section 4

- What kind of wave is the lecturer talking about in this section?

  _____

- Label the diagram.

Diagram 3

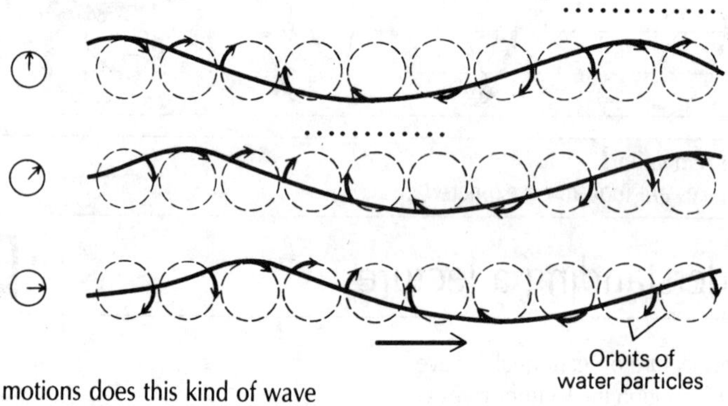

Orbits of
water particles

- What motions does this kind of wave involve?

  _____
  _____

Section 5

- Which waves travel through the earth?

  _____

- How does the other kind of wave travel?

  _____

- Label the diagram.

Diagram 4

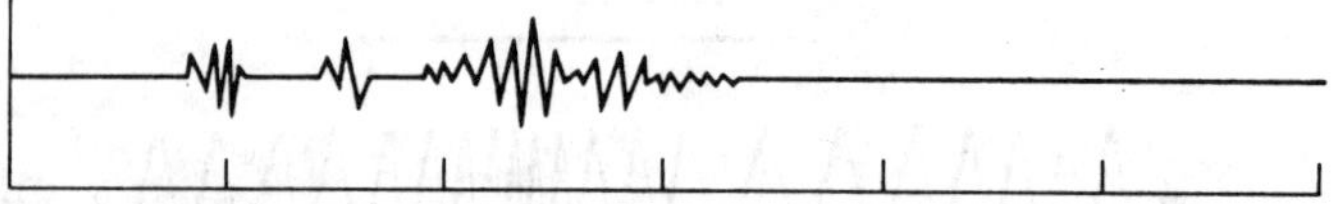

Now listen to the lecture again and take notes. When you have done that, write a summary of the lecture. Your answers to the questions and your notes will help you.

F. Understanding a printed text (2)

Read the following text carefully, looking up anything you do not understand.

THE EARTH'S INTERIOR

1 In Chap. 1 we saw that the average density of the earth as a whole is twice that of the crust. Evidently the earth cannot be hollow (as was once thought) or even like the crust but must consist of extremely dense materials. What are they likely to be? Are they solid or liquid? Is the interior a uniform mass or does it have a structure of some sort? Is it hot or cold? Answers exist for these questions which, though based on indirect arguments and leaving many details unsettled, nevertheless fit together into a reasonably complete picture of the inside of our planet.

Interior Structure

2   Earthquake P and S waves do not travel in straight lines within the earth. There are two reasons for this. The first is that the speeds of both kinds of waves increase with depth, so that their paths are somewhat curved owing to refraction. The second reason is more spectacular: there are layers of materials having different properties within the earth. When an earthquake wave traveling in one layer reaches the boundary, or *discontinuity*, that separates it from another layer in which its speed is different, refraction also occurs. Now, however, the refracted wave shows an abrupt change in direction, unlike the more gradual change due to speed variations within each layer.

Why P and S waves do not have straight paths

3   Let us suppose that an earthquake occurs somewhere. We consult the various seismological observatories and find that most though not all of them have recorded P waves from this event. Curiously, the stations that did not detect any P waves all lie along a band from 103° to 143° (11,400 to 15,900 km) distant from the earthquake. We would find, if we consulted the records of other earthquakes, that no matter where they took place, similar *shadow zones* existed. This is the clue that confirmed an early suspicion that the earth's interior is made up of concentric layers.

Shadow zones

4   Figure 8.11 shows why this conclusion is necessary. In the diagram the earth is divided into a central *core* and a surrounding *mantle*. P waves leaving the earthquake are able to go directly through the mantle only to a limited region slightly larger than a hemisphere. Those P waves that impinge upon the core are bent sharply toward the center of the earth, and, when they emerge, they are 4,500 km or more away from those P waves that just barely cleared the core. From an accurate analysis of the available data, it was found that the mantle is 2,900 km (1,800 mi) thick, which means that the core has

The earth has a central liquid core and an outer solid mantle

▼

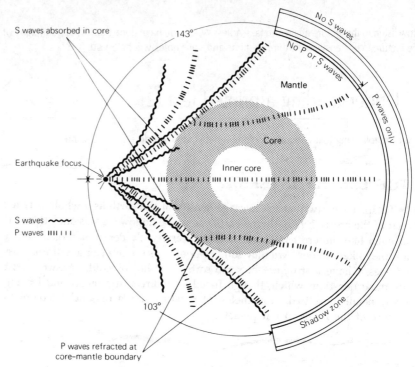

Fig. 8.11 How earthquake waves travel through the earth. The existence of a shadow zone between 103° and 143° where neither P nor S waves arrive is evidence for a central core. The inability of S waves to get through the core suggests that it is liquid.

a radius of 3,470 km (2,160 mi), over half the earth's total radius. However, the core constitutes less than 20 percent of the earth's volume.

5   Supporting the above finding and giving further important information about the nature of the core is the behavior of the S waves, which require a solid medium for their passage. The transverse motion involved in such waves requires that each particle of the medium in which they occur drag with it adjacent particles, which is impossible in a liquid where each particle is not firmly attached to its neighbors. The back-and-forth motion involved in P waves, on the other hand, simply requires that each particle exert a push on the next one, which can happen as easily in a liquid as in a solid. Since it is found that S waves cannot get through the core at all, the conclusion follows that the core is a liquid. A liquid core not only accounts for the absence of S waves but also for the marked changes in the velocity of P waves when they enter and leave the core.

6   The division of the earth into a core and mantle was first suggested in 1906 by R. D. Oldham to explain the presence of shadow zones. Later very sensitive seismographs came into use which detected faint traces of P waves in the shadow zones, which should not have been able to get there at all. In 1936 Inge Lehmann proposed that within the liquid core there is a smaller solid inner core that can bend some of the P waves passing through it so that they reach the shadow zones. Subsequent research confirmed this notion and the inner core is now believed to have a radius of 1,250 km (780 mi). Thus the earth's interior has the structure shown in Fig. 8.12.

S waves cannot pass through the core, and hence it must be liquid

The inner core is solid

7   From observations first made on a 1909 earthquake it became clear that there is a distinct difference between the surface regions of the earth and the underlying mantle. The line of demarcation is known as the *Mohorovicic discontinuity*, after its discoverer. Under the oceans it is seldom much more than 5 km thick; under the continents it averages about 35 km, and it may reach 70 km under some mountain ranges (Fig. 8.13).

The crust of the earth is relatively thin

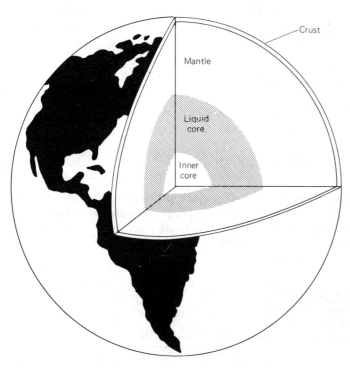

Fig. 8.12 Structure of the earth. The mantle constitutes 80 percent of the earth's volume and about 67 percent of its mass.

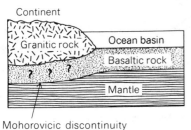

Fig. 8.13 General structure of the earth's crust.

G. Check your understanding

1. Look at the first paragraph again and say if this statement is correct or incorrect:

- There is direct and complete evidence to describe the earth's interior. ☐

2. Look at paragraph 2 again. Are these statements correct or incorrect?

- P and S waves travel at a fixed speed through any given layer of materials. ☐

- Refraction changes the direction in which the wave is travelling. ☐

3. Now look at paragraph 3 again. Can you explain what a *shadow zone* is?

4. Now look at paragraphs 4 and 5 again. Using the information given there, give a brief description of what Fig. 8.11 illustrates.

5. Now look at paragraph 6 again; choose the correct ending to this statement:

- Some P waves are able to reach the shadow zones because they are bent by:

  the mantle ☐
  the crust ☐
  the liquid core ☐
  the inner core ☐

H. Understanding discourse

Look at the four diagrams below, labelled 1 to 4. Then read through the four statements below them, labelled A to D. Now listen to a lecturer explaining the successive stages in the evolution of the Appalachian Mountains. As you listen, decide which statement belongs to which diagram. Also decide in which order the diagrams, with their accompanying statements, should appear.

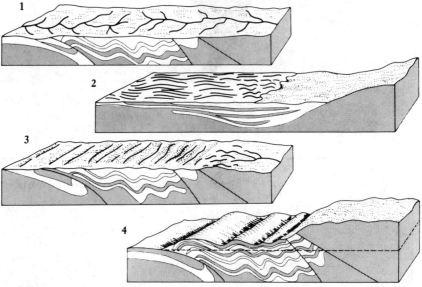

A. Original mountains worn down to a nearly level plain by stream erosion.

B. Sediments accumulating in the Appalachian basin.

C. Renewed erosion of the folded strata following vertical uplift, producing the parallel ridges and valleys of the present landscape.

D. Folding and thrust-faulting of rocks in the basin.

CONTINENTAL DRIFT

A. Understanding a printed text (1)

The following text will introduce you to the topic of **continental drift**. Look at the way it is divided into sections and paragraphs. Pay attention to the headings and notes in the margins, and to the illustrations and captions.

Now look at these questions:

1. What is the main idea in the first paragraph?
2. What was Wegener's suggestion?

3. What evidence is there for continental drift?
4. What was the weakness of Wegener's idea?
5. Is the idea of continental drift now accepted by geologists?

Read the passage through and find the answers to the questions. Remember, you do not have to understand every word to answer them.

CONTINENTAL DRIFT

1 A casual glance at a map of the world suggests the possibility that at some time in the past the continents were joined together in one or two giant supercontinents. If the margins of the continents are taken to be on their continental slopes (see Fig. 5.1) at a depth of 3,000 ft, instead of their present sea-level boundaries, the fit between North and South America, Africa, Greenland, and western Europe is remarkably exact, as Fig. 10.1 shows. But merely matching up outlines of continents is not by itself sufficient evidence that the continents have migrated around the globe. The first really comprehensive theory of continental drift was proposed early in this century by the German meteorologist Alfred Wegener, who based his argument on biologic and geologic evidence.

Wegener's Theory

2 At one time the standard explanation for the similarity of patterns of early life around the world was a series of land bridges linking the continents together. But this meant that the oceans were then separated from one another, so a series of channels had to be devised to permit aquatic plants and animals to pass between the oceans. No really believable scheme of bridges and channels could be devised, and even if one had been, it would still be necessary to account for the disappearance of all traces of them. Wegener was on firm ground when he searched for an alternative to this notion.

3 What Wegener suggested instead was that originally the continents were all part of a huge landmass he called Pangaea that was surrounded by a single ocean, Panthalassa. Pangaea then began to break up and the continents to slowly drift to their present locations. This model found additional support in geological data regarding prehistoric climates. At one time, South Africa, India, Australia, and part of South America were burdened with great ice sheets, while at the same time a tropical rain forest covered North America, Europe,

Wegener believed all the continents were once part of a single landmass

and China. At various other times, there was sufficient vegetation in Alaska and Antarctica for coal deposits to have resulted, and so currently frigid a place as Baffin Bay was a desert.

4   Wegener and his followers examined what was known about the climates of the distant past, and tried to arrange the continents in each geologic period so that the glaciers were near the poles and the hot regions were near the equator. The results, in general, were quite convincing, and in some cases startlingly so: deposits of glacial debris and fossil remains of certain distinctive plant species follow each other in the same succession in Argentina, Brazil, South Africa, Antarctica, India, and Australia, for example. A recent discovery of this kind was the identification of a skull of the reptile Lystrosaurus in a sandstone layer in the Alexandra mountain range of Antarctica. This creature, which was about three feet long, flourished long ago in Africa. It is as unlikely that Lystrosaurus swam the 2,700 mi between Africa and Antarctica as it is that a land bridge this long connected them, only to vanish completely later on.

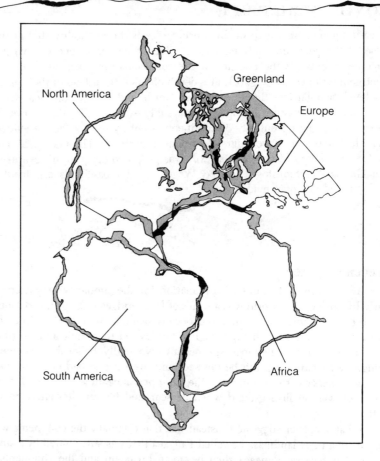

Fig. 10.1 How some of the continents fit together. The boundary of each continent is taken at a depth of 3,000 ft on its continental slope; the light gray regions represent land above sea level at present, and the dark gray regions represent submerged land on the continental shelf and slope. Overlaps are shown in black and gaps in white.

Laurasia and Gondwanaland

5   Today it seems almost certain that Pangaea did exist and later began to break apart into two supercontinents, *Laurasia* (which consisted of what is now North America, Greenland, and most of Eurasia) and *Gondwanaland* (South America, Africa, Antarctica, India, and Australia). Laurasia and Gondwanaland were almost equal in size (Fig. 10.2). The separation of Pagaea into these supercontinents is supported by detailed geological and biological evidence, for instance certain differences between Laurasian and Gondwanaland fossils of the same age.

Pangaea split into Laurasia and Gondwanaland

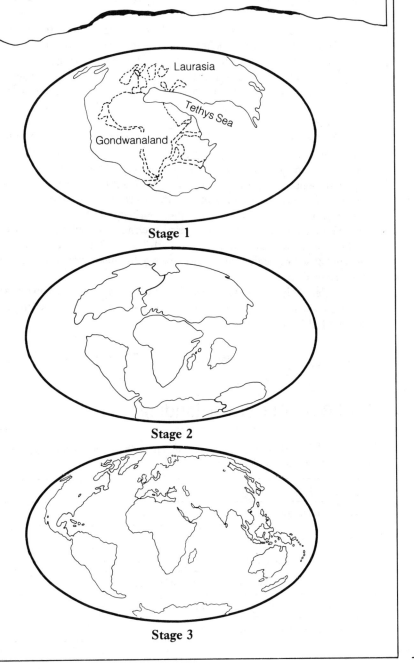

Stage 1

Stage 2

Stage 3

The Tethys Sea separated Laurasia and Gondwanaland

6   Laurasia and Gondwanaland were separated by a body of water called the *Tethys Sea*. Today a little of the Tethys Sea survives as the Mediterranean, Caspian, and Black Seas, but its original extent can be gauged from the sediments that were subsequently uplifted to form the mountain ranges that stretch from Gibraltar eastward to the Pacific. The Pyrenees, Alps, and Caucasus of Europe, the Atlas Mountains of North Africa, and the Himalayas of Asia all were once part of the Tethys Sea.

7   Not long after Pangaea split apart, South America and Africa became detached as a unit from the rest of Gondwanaland, and later they separated as the South Atlantic Ocean came into being. At a later date the Atlantic Ocean completed its extension northward, Australia separated from Antarctica, and India began to drift toward Asia.

8   The geologic processes responsible for continental drift are on such a huge scale that it is hard to believe they began relatively recently in the history of the earth. Hence it is likely that continental drift was taking place even before Pangaea was formed, and in fact there is some evidence that Pangaea was the result of the coming together of three earlier landmasses, Gondwanaland, Asia east of the Ural Mountains, and a unit consisting of North America, Greenland, and Europe.

9   Continental drift, then, has some very attractive aspects. Why was it not widely accepted until very recently? Wegener, who lacked a knowledge of the mechanical properties of the various parts of the earth's crust, envisioned the continents as floating freely over the mantle and having no trouble in moving *through* the ocean floors. If this were the case, only relatively weak forces would be needed to move the continents over the face of the earth, and Wegener was able to cite several such forces. But the ocean floors are in fact extremely hard and strong, and if enough force could somehow be applied, it seems likely that a continent would buckle rather than pass through the ocean floor.

10   An entirely different mechanism has proved to be involved, and until its discovery in the middle 1960s continental drift, for all its allure, remained discredited by most geologists.

The ocean floors are too hard and rigid for the continents to move through them

B. Check your understanding

1. Now read the text again carefully, looking up anything you do not understand. Then answer the following questions.

1. What does Fig. 10.1 show?

2. What explanation was the accepted one before Wegener's theory?

3. Why was this explanation not credible?

4. What were Pangaea and Panthalassa?

5. What evidence did Wegener have for this theory?

6. Why is the discovery of the Lystrosaurus skull significant?

7. Which supercontinent did your country once belong to?

8. What is the evidence for the existence of the two supercontinents?

9. Does the Tethys Sea still exist?

10. How did Wegener see the continents moving?

C. Increase your vocabulary

1. Look at the first paragraph and say which words have the opposite meaning to:

- taken apart
- careful
- stay in one place
- incomplete

2. Now look at paragraph 2 and say which words have the same meaning as:

- living in water
- explain
- idea
- joining
- usual

3. Now look at paragraph 3 and try to explain the following:

- drift
- ice sheet
- prehistoric
- tropical rain forest
- vegetation

4. Now look at paragraph 4 and say which words have the same meaning as:

- persuasive
- surprisingly
- alive and active
- disappear

5. Now look at paragraphs 5 and 6 again; then write sentences that show you know the meaning of:

- fossil
- gauge
- subsequent

6. Now look at paragraph 7 again; say what the following words refer to:

- line 2: they
- line 4: its

7. Now look at paragraph 8 again; what word has the same meaning as:

- therefore

8. Now look at paragraph 9 again; say what the following words refer to:

- line 1: it
- line 5: this
- line 7: such

D. Check your grammar

> **Do you remember?**
> Some verbs must be followed by the -ing form:
> He admitted *taking* my book.
> Some verbs must be followed by the infinitive:
> He agreed *to lend* me his book.

1. Make sentences from the following notes. Think whether you should use the infinitive *to* or the *-ing* form after the verbs.

- He/suggest/read/chapter 5/before/we/go/ lecture.
- He/want/spend/more time/study.
- The continents/continue/drift/today.
- Wegener/try/find/alternative explanation.
- I/enjoy/listen/music.
- I/prevent/study/noise next door.

- He/not mind/work/weekends.
- I/not want/risk/fail/my exams.
- He/forget/hand in/essay/last night.
- There/nothing/that shop/worth/buy.
- It/no use/leave/your work/last minute.
- I/miss/watch/the university football match/last week.
- He/hope/get/good result/his examinations.
- I/expect/go/home/holidays.
- I/stop/work/later this evening.

2. Make nouns from the following adjectives, using *-ness* or *-ability*:

- complete
- useful
- comparable
- suitable
- soluble
- vast
- divisible
- wet
- reasonable
- responsible

E. Understanding a lecture

Listen to this lecture introducing plate tectonics. Using the information the lecturer gives you, answer the questions below. The lecture is divided into sections.

Section 1

- How did Wegener think the continents move?

- What does the lecturer say about the ocean floors?

- How does plate tectonics see the movement of continents?

Section 2

- How does the lecturer describe the crust of the earth?

- What is the layer near the top of the mantle capable of?

Section 3

- What is the term the lecturer gives to the shell?

- How thick is it?

- What is the term given to the softer region?

- How thick is it?

Section 4

- Complete the following statement:

  The difference in seismic-wave speed suggests that the minerals in the mantle and the crust are different

  in _____

  or _____

  or _____

- Are these statements correct or incorrect?

  The asthenosphere is distinguished from the lithosphere by its rigidity.   ☐

  The asthenosphere responds like a thick, viscous fluid when a brief force is applied to it.   ☐

Now listen to the lecture again and take notes. When you have done that, write a summary of the lecture. Your answers to the questions and your notes will help you.

F. Understanding a printed text (2)

Read the following text carefully, looking up anything you do not understand.

The Ocean Floors

1 The mountains and valleys, plains and plateaus of the continents have been known for a long time, and few surprises are in store for future explorers. But the continents occupy less than 30 percent of the area of the earth's crust, while the rest lies hidden in perpetual darkness thousands of meters below the seas and oceans. Only in the past 2 decades have the floors of the oceans been mapped and their physical characters elucidated. It is largely these findings that have clarified the evolution of the crust.

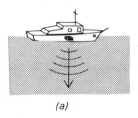
(a)
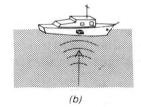
(b)

Fig. 10.4 The principle of echo sounding. (*a*) A pulse of high-frequency sound waves is sent out by a suitable device on a ship. (*b*) The time at which the pulse returns to the ship is a measure of the sea depth.

2 The methods used to investigate the ocean floors are not particularly subtle—the real problem has been the vastness of the area to be covered. These days depths are charted by means of echo sounders: such an instrument sends out a pulse of high-frequency sound waves, and the time needed for it to reach the seafloor, be reflected there, and then to return to the surface is a measure of how deep the water is (Fig. 10.4). A variant of this method reveals something of the structure of the seafloor itself. What is done is to detonate an explosive charge in the water and study the returning echoes—one echo will come from the top of the sediment layer, and a later one from the hard rock underneath. Samples of the seafloor can be obtained by dropping a hollow tube to the bottom on a long cable and then pulling it up filled with a core of the sediments into which it sank. These sediments can be examined later in the laboratory for their composition, their age, as well as, of course, the fossils they contain, their magnetization, and so forth. Another important technique is to tow a magnetometer behind a survey ship to obtain an idea of the direction and intensity of the magnetization of the rocks of the ocean floor over wide areas.

Echo sounding

3 Four findings about ocean floors have proved of crucial importance:

1 The ocean floors are, geologically speaking, very young.

2 A worldwide system of narrow ridges and somewhat broader *rises* runs across the oceans (Fig. 10.5). An example is the Mid-Atlantic Ridge, which virtually bisects the Atlantic Ocean from north to south; Iceland, the Azores, Ascension Island, and Tristan da Cunha are some of the higher peaks in this ridge. These ridges are offset at intervals by fracture zones that indicate transverse shifts of the ocean floors.

3 There is also a system of *trenches* several kilometers deep that rims the Pacific Ocean. These trenches parallel the belts in which most of today's earthquakes and volcanoes occur and usually have *island arcs* on their landward sides that consist of volcanic mountains projecting above sea level.

4 The direction in which ocean-floor rocks are magnetized is the same along strips parallel to the midocean ridges, but the direction is reversed from strip to strip going away from a ridge on either side (Fig. 10.6).

The ocean floors are relatively young

Oceanic ridges and rises

Oceanic trenches and island arcs

Magnetization of the ocean floors

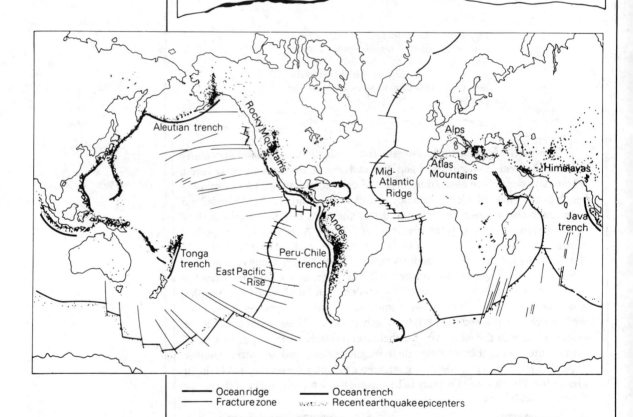

| Ocean ridge | Ocean trench |
| Fracture zone | Recent earthquake epicenters |

Fig. 10.5 The worldwide system of oceanic ridges and trenches. The ridges are offset by transverse fracture zones. Color dots represent epicenters of earthquakes recorded from 1957 to 1967.

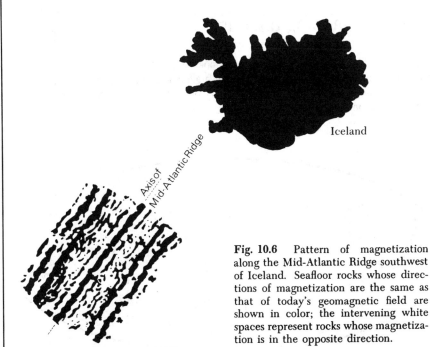

Iceland

Axis of Mid-Atlantic Ridge

Fig. 10.6 Pattern of magnetization along the Mid-Atlantic Ridge southwest of Iceland. Seafloor rocks whose directions of magnetization are the same as that of today's geomagnetic field are shown in color; the intervening white spaces represent rocks whose magnetization is in the opposite direction.

G. Check your understanding

1. Look at the first paragraph and say whether these statements are correct or incorrect:

- There is little more to be learnt about the earth's landmasses. ☐
- Studies of the ocean floors have contributed to our understanding of the earth's crust. ☐

2. Look at paragraph 2 and complete the following statement correctly:

- The difficulties in studying the ocean floors are caused by

  the time it takes ☐
  the simplicity of the equipment ☐
  the size of the area to be studied ☐
  the use of echo sounders ☐

3. Are these statements correct or incorrect?

- Explosive charges are used to study the structure of the seafloor. ☐
- A magnetometer is used to collect samples from the seafloor. ☐

4. Now look at paragraph 2 again and say what these words refer to:

- line 3: such
- line 5: it
- line 7: itself
- line 11: it
- line 12: it

5. Now look at paragraph 4 and say whether these statements are correct or incorrect:

- The four findings are not really very significant. ☐
- The terms ridge and rise are interchangeable. ☐
- Trenches are not found in the Atlantic Ocean. ☐
- Ocean-floor rocks are always magnetised in the same direction. ☐

H. Understanding discourse

A lecturer is talking about what the earth may look like 30 million years from now, if the continents continue to drift in the way that they are today. Using the picture below, note down the changes that he mentions. Then say what other changes you notice that the lecturer does not mention.

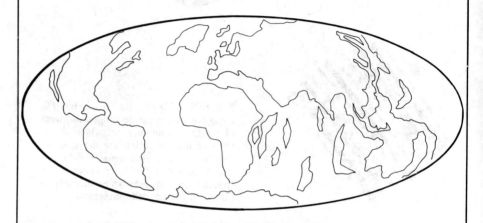

Fig. 10.13 How the earth may appear in 30 million years from now if present trends continue.

THE SOLAR SYSTEM (1)

A. Understanding a printed text (1)

The following text will introduce you to the topic of the **solar system**. Look at the way it is divided into sections and paragraphs. Pay attention to the headings and notes in the margins, and to the illustrations and captions.

Now look at these questions:

1. What is the solar system?
2. How many planets are there?

3. What is the difference between Fig. 12.1 and Fig. 12.2?
4. Why do planets shine?

Read the passage through and find the answers to the questions. Remember, you do not have to understand every word to answer them.

To the largest modern telescope as to the naked eye, a star is no more than a tiny point of light. Most of the planents, on the other hand, are magnified to clear disks by a telescope of even modest power. This does not mean that the planets are larger than the stars, of course, but only that they are much closer to us. If we use a golf ball to represent the sun, a small sand grain a dozen feet away represents the earth on the same scale. Pluto would be another sand grain 500 ft from the golf ball. Within the 1,000-ft-wide orbit of Pluto are all the other planets. In this model, the nearest star would be another golf ball 600 mi away.

The earth and the sun and the other eight planets are isolated in space. This set of nine spheres that circle the bright sun is poised in emptiness and separated by unimaginable distances from everything else in the universe. Because the sun is its central figure, the family of bodies that accompanies it is called the *solar system*, and in this chapter we shall survey briefly what is known about its members.

THE FAMILY OF THE SUN

3 Until the seventeenth century the solar system was thought to consist of only five planets besides the earth and moon. In 1609, soon after having heard of the invention of the telescope in Holland, Galileo built one of his own and was able to add four new bodies to the system: the brighter of the moons (or *satellites*) that revolve around Jupiter. Since Galileo's time telescopic improvements have made possible the discovery of many more members of the sun's family,

There are nine planets in orbits around the sun

The list of planets now includes nine; in order from the sun they are Mercury, Venus, Earth, Mars, Jupiter, Saturn, Uranus, Neptune, and Pluto (Fig. 12.1). All except Mercury, Venus, and Pluto have satellites. Thousands of small objects called *asteroids*, all less than 500 mi in diameter, follow separate orbits about the sun in the region between Mars and Jupiter. Comets and meteors, in Galileo's time thought to be atmospheric phenomena, are now recognized as still smaller members of the solar system.

The Solar System

4   Not only is the entire solar system isolated in space, but each of its principal members is separated from the others by vast distances. From the earth to our nearest neighbor, the moon, is about 238,000 mi; from the earth to the sun is about 93 million mi. It took the *Apollo 11* spacecraft 3 days to reach the vicinity of the moon, and at the same rate of progress more than 3 years would be needed to reach the sun.

5   Let us return for a moment to the model mentioned at the start of this chapter in which a golf ball represented the sun and a grain of sand 12 ft away the earth. On this scale the moon would be scarcely more than a dust speck about $\frac{1}{2}$ in from the sand grain. The largest planet, Jupiter, would be a small pebble 60 ft from the golf ball.

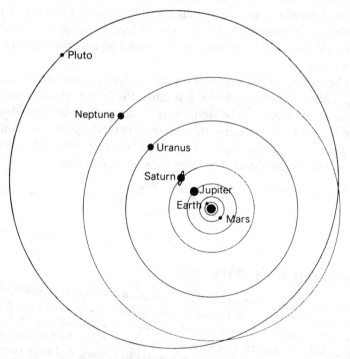

Fig. 12.1 The solar system. The orbits of Mercury and Venus are too small to be shown on this scale. Pluto's orbit is by far the most elliptical. Diameters of sun and planets are exaggerated.

With three smaller pebbles, three more sand grains, and a few more dust specks, all within the 1,000-ft-wide orbit of Pluto, the model is complete (Fig. 12.2). An extremely empty structure, this solar system, with its members separated by distances enormous compared with their size.

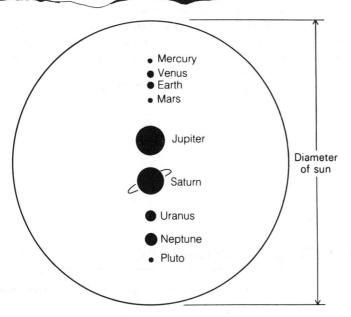

Fig. 12.2 Relative sizes of planets and sun.

6   Planets *revolve* around the sun and *rotate* on their axes. Two further aspects of the solar system are notable:

1   Nearly all the revolutions and rotations are in the same direction, which is counterclockwise as seen looking down from above the North Pole. Only the rotation of Venus and the revolutions of a few satellites are in the opposite direction. Uranus is an exception of a different kind, since it rotates about an axis only 8° from the plane of its orbit.

2   All the orbits except those of the comets lie nearly in the same plane (Fig. 12.3).

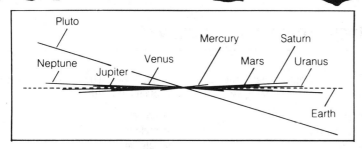

Fig. 12.3 The orbits of the planets seen edgewise; they lie nearly in the same plane.

7 Planets, asteroids, and satellites are visible by virtue of the sunlight they reflect. What we see of any of these objects at a particular time is limited to the half that faces the sun. Planets with orbits larger than that of the earth never come between us and the sun, so we can always see nearly the whole of their illuminated sides. Mercury and Venus, however, have orbits smaller than the earth's and are between us and the sun for a good part of each revolution. In this position their dark sides are turned toward us, and we see them either not at all or as crescents.

B. Check your understanding

Now read the text again, looking up anything you do not understand. Then answer the following questions:

1. What does the writer use to represent the sun in his model?

2. In the model, how far away is Pluto?

3. What did Galileo discover?

4. What is an asteroid?

5. What is the distance from the earth to the sun?

6. In the model, how large is the moon?

7. How do planets move?

8. Which planets do not come between the earth and the sun?

C. Increase your vocabulary

1. Look at paragraphs 1 and 2 and say which have the same meaning as:

- very small
- on its/their own
- made bigger
- sphere

2. Now look at paragraph 3 again and try to explain the words:

- comet
- meteor
- satellite
- asteroid

3. Now look at paragraph 5 and again explain the difference between:

- speck
- grain
- pebble

4. Now look at paragraphs 6 and 7 again. Write sentences that show you know the meanings of:

- rotate
- revolve
- counterclockwise
- illuminate
- crescent
- orbit

5. Now use your dictionary and complete the following table:

Verb	Noun	Adjective
revolve		
	invention	
	system	
rotate		
	circle	
represent		

D. Check your grammar

Make complete sentences out of the following notes, putting the verbs in brackets in the right tense. Then arrange the sentences into two paragraphs. Make sure that each paragraph makes sense, and that the sentences follow each other logically. Start with the heading:

METEORS

- meteoroids/through/atmosphere/rapidly/swiftly/the/by/friction

  (*move; heat*)

- so/substantial/sometimes/large/that/a/surface/to/they/to begin with/the/earth's/portion

  (*be; get through*)

- tons/these/dustlike/planet/daily/of/many/fine/micrometeorites/our

  (*reach*)

- random/occurrence/of/in/meteors/these/most

  (*be*)

- following/showers/when/the/swarm/meteors/of/a/earth/the/through/orbit/about/same/the/sun/the

  (*come about; move*)

- fragments/matter/earth/the/small/as it travels/space/meteoroids/that/of/through

  (*be; meet*)
  _____

- largest/meteorites/fallen/tons/the/known/meteoroids/several/called

  (*weigh*)
  _____

- October 19–23/year/May 4–6/conspicuous/the/meteor showers/about/August 10–14/ every/most/and

  (*can see*)
  _____

- average/clear/many/a/observer/an/an/keen/hour/on/night/as/10 meteors/as

  (*can spot*)
  _____

- completely/streaks/the/60 mi/the/usually/in/bright/earth/above/they/as/sky/about

  (*burn up; appear*)
  _____

- masses/a/less/most/gram/meteoroids/of/than

  (*have*)
  _____

- smallest/atmosphere/that/through/burning up/meteoroids/so/the/they/light/the/without

  (*be; float*)
  _____

- pattern/or/place/they/no/either/the/time/particular/in/the/that/they/sky/in

  (*follow; appear*)
  _____

- of/several/with/100/visible/50/per/to/meteor showers/at/specific/year/more/or/hour/great/ meteors/times

  (*occur*)
  _____

E. Understanding a lecture

Listen to this lecture on comets. Using the information the lecturer gives you, answer the questions below. The lecture is divided into sections. Listen to each section twice.

Section 1—————————————

- Complete the statement correctly.

  The lecturer says that you:

  must read more about comets. ☐
  need not read more about comets unless you want to. ☐
  must not read more about comets at this stage. ☐

- Are these statements correct or incorrect?

  Comets can only be seen through telescopes. ☐

  The comet's tail does not increase in size as it approaches. ☐

Section 2—————————————

- What kind of path do the planets follow?
  _____

- Is this statement correct or incorrect?

  A comet's path is usually a long, narrow ellipse. ☐

- When do comets return?
  _____

- Which comet returns every 76 years?
  _____

- Note down the main reason why comets can only be seen when they are close to the sun.

  _____
  _____

- Note down the second reason.

  _____
  _____

- Is this statement correct or incorrect?

  One reason why a comet's tail points away from the sun is the pressure of the sun's radiation pushing gases from the head of the comet. □

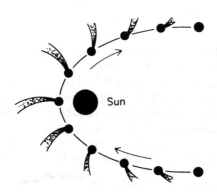

Diagram 1

- The lecturer gives 5 components of comets. What are they?

  _____
  _____
  _____
  _____

- How wide are the comet heads?

  _____

- Is this statement correct or incorrect?

  When a comet disintegrates it forms swarms of meteoroids. □

Now listen to the lecture again and take notes. When you have done that, write a summary of the lecture. Your answers to the questions and your notes will help you.

F. Understanding a printed text (2)

Read the following text carefully, looking up anything you do not understand.

THE PLANETS

1 The planets seem to fall naturally into two categories. The *inner planets* of Mercury, Venus, Earth, and Mars are solid, relatively small, and rotate fairly slowly on their axes. The *outer planets* of Jupiter, Saturn, Uranus, and Neptune are gaseous, large, and rotate fairly rapidly. Although relatively little is known about Pluto, it seems to resemble the inner planets more than the outer ones despite its status as the outermost one of all.

Mercury

Mercury is the smallest planet

2   Mercury, smallest of the planets, has a crater-pocked surface much like that of the moon but lacking the extensive lava flows so prominent there. The *Mariner 10* spacecraft detected a weak magnetic field around Mercury but no atmosphere. A bleak place, but an interesting one because the combination of a high density and little surface melting in the past suggests a quite different geologic history from that of the earth. Surface temperatures on the sunlit side are 300° C or so, and because there is no atmosphere to transfer or retain heat, the temperature drops at night to about −175° C.

Venus

Venus rotates "backwards" very slowly

3   In size and mass the planet Venus resembles the earth more closely than any other member of the sun's family. Apart from the sun and the moon, Venus is the brightest object in the sky, and is even visible in daylight. Venus has the distinction of spinning "backward" on its axis; that is, looking downward on its north pole, Venus rotates clockwise, whereas the earth and the other planets rotate counterclockwise. The rotation of Venus is extremely slow, so that a "day" on that planet represents 243 of our days.

Venus is too hot to support life

4   The surface of Venus is obscured by thick layers of clouds. The dense atmosphere is mainly carbon dioxide, with a little nitrogen and a trace of water vapor also present. At the surface, atmospheric pressure is a hundred times that of the earth. On the earth carbon dioxide is an important absorber of radiation from the earth that prevents the rapid loss of heat from the ground after sunset. Venus, blanketed more effectively by far than the earth, retains more heat; estimates based on data radioed back by spacecraft suggest an average surface temperature of about 430°C, enough to melt lead. Since the temperature is so high, the existence of life on Venus seems impossible.

Mars

5   The reddish planet Mars has long fascinated astronomers and laymen alike, for it is the only other known body on which surface conditions seemed suitable for life of some kind. Yet Martian climates are exceedingly severe by our standards, and the thin atmosphere does little to screen solar ultraviolet radiation. If life exists on Mars, it is adapted to an environment that would soon destroy most earthly organisms.

6   Mars rotates on its axis in a little over 24 h; its revolution about the sun requires nearly 2 years; and its axis is inclined to the plane of its orbit at nearly the same angle as the earth's. These facts mean that the Martian day and night have about the same lengths as ours and that Martian seasons are 6 months long and at least as pronounced as ours. Over half again farther from the sun than the earth, Mars receives considerably less light and heat. Its atmosphere, largely carbon dioxide, is extremely thin, so little of the sun's heat is retained after nightfall. Daytime temperatures in summer rise to perhaps 30°C, but at nightfall drop to perhaps −75°C.

7   Another difficulty that life must face on Mars is the scarcity of water. A trifle is certainly there, as water vapor in the atmosphere and possibly in the white polar caps as well, but apparently not a great deal. The polar caps, which increase in area in winter and decrease in area in summer, are believed to be almost entirely frozen carbon dioxide ("dry ice"). However, water may well have once been more abundant on Mars than it is today. Some surface features photographed by the *Mariner* 9 spacecraft early in 1972 strongly suggest erosion by running water within the past million years or so. The earth's surface water probably was vented from volcanoes early in its history, and there seems no reason why the same process should not have occurred on Mars, whose surface is dotted with extinct volcanoes.

8   The fact that most terrestrial life requires liquid water and oxygen plus protection from solar ultraviolet radiation does not necessarily mean that life of some kind could not develop in their absence. Certain bacteria on the earth are known whose life processes require carbon dioxide, not oxygen, so an oxygen-containing atmosphere is not indispensable, at least for primitive forms of life. Conceivably organisms could exist which can thrive on water gleaned from traces of it in the minerals of surface rocks. And shells of some sort might protect Martian creatures from ultraviolet radiation. The absence of indications of life in photographs taken thousands of miles away from the Martian surface is in itself not significant; at such distances terrestrial life would probably not be apparent to a visitor from elsewhere. (And a closer look might suggest that the car is the most conspicuous form of life on earth.)

9   The pictures radioed back by *Mariner 9* as it orbited Mars showed a host of intriguing geologic structures, many apparently of recent origin. The Martian landscape is extremely varied: there are regions pocked with huge craters, regions broken up into irregular short ridges and depressions, vast lava flows, channels that look as though they were carved by running water, even peculiar areas that seem to indicate glacial activity. Though rainstorms are absent—at least these days—violent winds periodically drive great clouds of dust around the planet. The surface markings so obvious through the telescope do not seem to coincide with the topographical features found by *Mariner 9,* and some of these markings are known to change color with the Martian seasons. Perhaps the dust storms also follow the seasons and are responsible for the color changes; perhaps some form of vegetation is the cause; perhaps the true explanation lies elsewhere.

10   Early in this century the Italian astronomer Giovanni Schiaparelli and the American Percival Lowell reported that the surface of Mars was covered with networks of fine lines, popularly called canals (a poor English translation of the Italian *canali,* meaning "channels"). The apparent straightness and geometric patterns of these canals were considered evidence of the work of intelligent beings. But the pictures radioed back by the various spacecraft to pass near Mars show no signs of canals, though there do seem to be several regions where a number of craters are approximately in line. Probably the canals are optical illusions; certainly the existence of Martian creatures advanced enough to be capable of digging actual canals is highly unlikely.

G. Check your understanding

1. Look at the first paragraph again. Are these statements correct or incorrect?

- The inner planets rotate at a slower speed than the outer planets. ☐
- Pluto is similar to Jupiter. ☐

2. Now look at paragraph 2. Are these statements correct or incorrect?

- Mercury does not resemble the moon in any way. ☐
- The geologic history of Mercury is similar to that of the earth. ☐

3. Now look at paragraph 3 again. Are these statements correct or incorrect?

- You can see Venus during the daytime. ☐
- Venus spins in the same way as the earth. ☐

4. Now look at paragraph 4 again. Are these statements correct or incorrect?

- There is no water vapour in Venus' atmosphere. ☐
- Venus loses heat more rapidly than the earth. ☐

5. Now look at paragraph 5 again. Is this statement correct or incorrect?

- There is no atmosphere round Mars. ☐

6. Now look at paragraph 6 again. Are these statements correct or incorrect?

- Night and day on Mars are very similar in length to the earth's. ☐
- Mars does not get as much heat or light as the earth. ☐

7. Now look at paragraph 7 again. Are these statements correct or incorrect?

- There is no water on Mars. ☐
- There have certainly never been streams or rivers on Mars. ☐

8. Now look at paragraph 8 again. Are these statements correct or incorrect?

- All living organisms require oxygen. ☐
- The writer thinks it possible that there may be some form of life on Mars. ☐

9. Now look at paragraph 9 again. Are these statements correct or incorrect?

- The Martian landscape is very much the same all over the planet. ☐
- Mariner 9 found the same features on Mars as have been seen through telescopes. ☐

10. Now look at paragraph 10 again. Is this statement correct or incorrect?

- Spacecraft have confirmed the existence of channels on Mars. ☐

H. Understanding discourse

Look at the four pictures of Mars radioed back to earth by Mariner 9 in 1972. Then read the statements below the pictures. As you listen to the lecturer match the pictures to the statements.

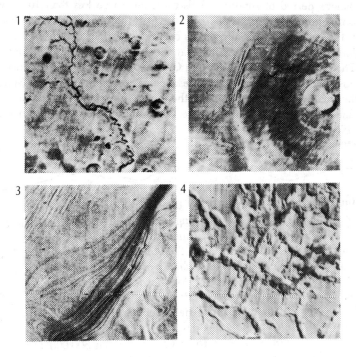

A. A relatively smooth region that seems to have been deposited in layers.

B. A chaotic landscape with no terrestrial equivalent.

C. A volcano on the Tharis Ridge.

D. A channel that seems to have been cut by moving liquid.

UNIT 14

THE SOLAR SYSTEM (2)

A. Understanding a printed text (1)

The following text continues the topic of the **solar system**. Look at the way it is divided into sections and paragraphs. Pay attention to the headings and notes in the margins, and to the illustration.

Now look at these questions:

1. What are the main points, such as size, composition and so on, that the writer makes about Jupiter?

2. What are the main points that the writer makes about Saturn?

3. What are the main points the writer makes about Uranus, Neptune and Pluto?

Read the passage through and find the answers to the questions. Remember, you do not have to understand every word to answer them.

Jupiter

Jupiter rotates very rapidly

1   The giant planet Jupiter, like Venus, is shrouded in clouds. The clouds occur in bands of changing color—yellow, red, brown, blue, purple, gray—and there are some semipermanent markings, such as the Red Spot some tens of thousands of kilometers across. The latter make possible a determination of the planet's period of rotation. This turns out to be less than 10 h, which means that points on Jupiter's equator travel at the enormous speed of 45,000 km/h; the earth's equatorial speed is only 1,670 km/h. Because of its rapid rotation, Jupiter bulges much more at the equator than the earth does.

2   The four satellites of Jupiter that Galileo discovered over 3 centuries ago are conspicuous objects in a small telescope. The largest is as big as Mercury, and the smallest is about the size of the moon. The other eight satellites are very small (25 to 250 km in diameter), and one of them escaped detection until 1951.

Jupiter, Saturn, Uranus, and Neptune are composed chiefly of hydrogen and helium

3   Jupiter's volume is about 1,300 times that of the earth, but its mass is only 300 times as great. The resulting low density—only a third more than that of water—means that Jupiter cannot be composed of a mixture of rock, iron, and nickel as is the earth. Like the other giant planets (Saturn, Uranus, and Neptune), Jupiter must consist chiefly of hydrogen and helium, the two lightest elements. Probably Jupiter does not have an actual surface; instead, its atmosphere gradually becomes thicker and thicker with increasing depth until it becomes a liquid. A terrestrial analogy might be the slushy surface of a snowbank on a warm winter day.

4   Jupiter's interior is believed to be very hot, about 500,000°C according to some estimates, but not hot enough for nuclear reactions to occur in its hydrogen content whose release of energy would turn Jupiter into a star. But if Jupiter's mass were 30 times greater, the increased internal pressure would push the temperature to 20 million°C, and the result would be a miniature star.

5   Jupiter's atmosphere apparently contains such gases as ammonia, methane, and water vapor as well as hydrogen and helium. As mentioned earlier, laboratory experiments show that when a mixture of these gases is exposed to energy sources such as are usually present in a planetary atmosphere (for instance lightning, ultraviolet light, streams of fast ions), the various organic compounds characteristic of life are formed. It seems entirely possible—some biologists think probable—that some form of life has evolved in the dense lower atmosphere of Jupiter. It is interesting that simple microorganisms such as bacteria and yeasts are able to survive when exposed to gas mixtures that simulate the Jovian atmosphere at temperatures and pressures comparable to those on Jupiter.

Life of some kind may exist in Jupiter's atmosphere

6   The American spacecraft *Pioneer 10* passed close to Jupiter late in 1973 after a journey that lasted 20 months and covered over a billion kilometers. Of the wealth of information radioed back, a few items are especially notable. For example, Jupiter has a complex magnetic field about 8 times stronger than the earth's, and this field traps high-energy protons and electrons from the sun in belts that extend many Jovian radii outward. (The *Van Allen belts* around the earth are similar, but 10,000 times weaker.) Another important finding confirmed that Jupiter radiates over twice as much energy as it receives from the sun, which means that it has powerful internal sources of energy; by contrast, the atmospheres of Venus, Earth, and Mars are in balance, and radiate only as much energy as they get from the sun. It has been suggested that Jupiter is still contracting gravitationally, and in this contraction potential energy is turned into heat just as compressing air in a tire pump warms up the air.

Jupiter has a strong magnetic field and radiates more energy than it receives

Saturn

7   In its setting of brilliant rings, Saturn is the most beautiful of the earth's kindred. The planet itself is much like Jupiter: similarly flattened at the poles by rapid rotation, similarly possessing a dense atmosphere, its surface similarly hidden by banded clouds. Farther from the sun than Jupiter, Saturn is considerably colder; ammonia is largely frozen out of its atmosphere, and its clouds consist mostly of methane.

8   The famous rings, two bright ones and a fainter inner one, surround the planet in the plane of its equator. This plane is somewhat inclined to Saturn's orbit. Hence, as Saturn moves in its leisurely 29-year journey around the sun, we see the rings from different angles. Twice in the 29-year period the rings are edgewise to the earth; in this position they are practically invisible, which suggests that their thickness is small, perhaps 20 km as compared with the 270,000-km diameter of the outer ring.

Saturn's rings consist of small solid bodies in orbits around it

9   The rings are not the solid sheets they appear to be but instead consist of myriad small bodies ranging in size from boulders a meter or more across to dust particles, each of which revolves about Saturn like a miniature satellite. No satellite of substantial size can exist close to its parent planet because

Saturn.

of the disruptive effect of tide-producing forces, which are proportionately less the farther distant the satellite. The *Roche limit* is the minimum radius that a satellite orbit must have if the satellite is to remain intact; the limit is named in honor of E. A. Roche, who investigated the origin of Saturn's rings a century ago. For Saturn the Roche limit is calculated to be 2.4 times the planet's radius, and in fact the outer rim of the outer ring is 2.3 radii from the center of Saturn and the closest satellite never approaches closer than 3.1 radii from the center. Saturn has 10 ordinary satellites outside the rings; the innermost of these was discovered in 1966.

The Roche limit

Uranus, Neptune, Pluto

10   The three outermost planets, Uranus, Neptune, and Pluto, owe their discovery to the telescope. Uranus was found quite by accident in 1781, during a systematic search of the sky by the great English astronomer William Herschel. It is just barely visible to the naked eye, and in fact had been identified as a faint star on a number of sky maps prepared during the preceding hundred years. Herschel suspected Uranus to be a planet because, through the telescope, it appeared as a disk rather than as a point of light. Observations made over a period of time showed its position to be changing relative to the stars, and its orbit was determined from these data. The discoveries of Neptune in 1846 and of Pluto in 1930 were made as the result of predictions based on their gravitational effects on other planets.

The existences of Neptune and Pluto were predicted before they were discovered

11   Uranus and Neptune are large bodies, each with a diameter about $3\frac{1}{2}$ times that of the earth. Pluto is somewhat smaller than Mars, and may once have been a satellite of Neptune that somehow was pulled away to pursue its own orbit around the sun. In most of their properties Uranus and Neptune resemble Jupiter and Saturn. Their atmospheres are largely methane, which accounts for their greenish color, with some hydrogen present as well. Because these planets are so far from the sun, their surface temperatures are below $-200°C$, and any ammonia present would be frozen out of their atmospheres. Pluto is so small, so far away, and so feebly illuminated that reliable information about it is difficult to obtain.

B. Check your understanding

Now read the text again, looking up anything you do not understand. Then answer the following questions:

1. What is the similarity between Jupiter and Venus?

2. How does Jupiter's speed compare with the earth's?

3. What kind of surface does Jupiter have?

4. Why do some biologists think life is possible on Jupiter?

5. How does Jupiter's magnetic field compare with the earth's?

6. Why is ammonia largely frozen out of Saturn's atmosphere?

7. What do Saturn's rings consist of?

8. What is the *Roche limit*?

9. Why did Herschel think Uranus was a planet?

10. In what ways are Uranus and Neptune similar to Jupiter and Saturn?

C. Increase your vocabulary

1. Look at the first paragraph and say what these words refer to:

- line 4: The latter
- line 5: this
- line 7: its

2. Look at the first paragraph again. What prefix, like un-, is used to mean half?

3. Now look at paragraphs 2 and 3 and say which words or expressions have the same meaning as:

- was not found
- as a consequence
- a comparison based on the earth

4. Now look at paragraphs 4 and 5 and say which words have approximately the same meaning as:

- so it would seem
- left uncovered or unprotected
- developed over a period of time
- small-scale
- very thick

5. Now look at paragraph 6 and say which words have the opposite meaning to:

- poverty
- unremarkable
- simple
- inward

6. Now look at paragraphs 7 and 8 again and explain the following words and expressions:

- in the plane of
- somewhat inclined
- edgewise

7. Now look at paragraph 9 and say which words have the opposite meaning to:

- small in number
- outermost
- broken up

8. Now look at paragraphs 10 and 11 and say which words have approximately the same meaning as:

- coming before
- follow
- a little bit
- in some way

D. Check your grammar

ASKING QUESTIONS AND PARAGRAPH WRITING
You have been asked to write three short paragraphs on *The Motions of the Moon*. Your teacher has the information you need to do this. Ask questions to get the information you need. You should illustrate what you write with the diagram below, which will need labelling. Your three paragraphs should deal with the following subjects.

1. The size of the moon.

2. How the moon moves round the earth.

3. The phases of the moon.

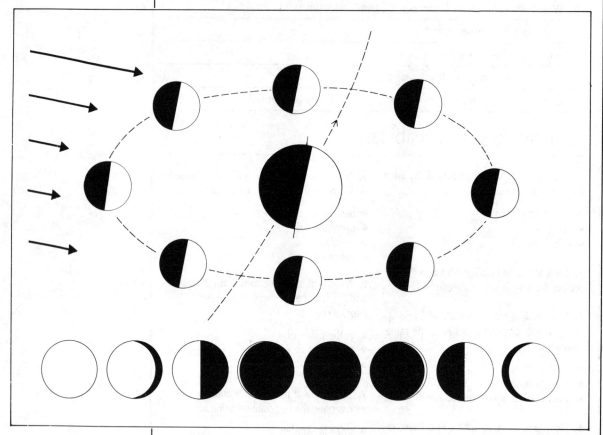

E. Understanding a lecture

Listen to this lecture on eclipses. Using the information the lecturer gives you, answer the questions below. The lecture is divided into sections. Listen to each section twice.

Section 1

• Note down the eight phases of the moon.

- When can we see a moon that is fully illuminated?

  ————————————————————

- When can we see nothing or very little of the moon?

  ————————————————————

Section 3————————————————

- What is the answer to the questions the lecturer raises?

  ————————————————————

  ————————————————————

Section 4————————————————

- When do eclipses occur?

  ————————————————————

Section 5————————————————

- What two kinds of eclipse are there?

  ————————————————————

  ————————————————————

- What is accounted for by the fact that the diameter of the sun and the moon appear the same from the earth?

  ————————————————————

Section 6————————————————

- Label the diagram.

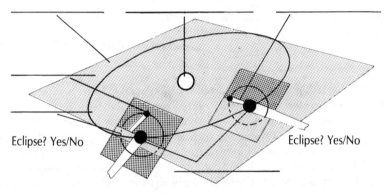

Eclipse? Yes/No   Eclipse? Yes/No

Now listen to the lecture again and take notes. When you have done that, write a summary of the lecture. Your answers to the questions and your notes will help you.

F. Understanding a printed text (2)

Read the following text carefully, looking up anything you do not understand.

The Lunar Surface

1   The moon was hardly a mystery even before the voyages of *Apollo 11* and of the other manned spacecraft that followed it there. Even a small telescope reveals the chief features of the lunar landscape: wide plains, jagged mountain ranges, and innumerable craters of all sizes. Each mountain stands out in vivid clarity, with no clouds or haze to hide the smallest detail. Mountain shadows are black and sharp-edged. When the moon passes before a star, the star remains bright and clear up to the moon's very edge. From these observations we conclude that the moon has little or no atmosphere. Water is likewise absent, as indicated by the complete lack of lakes, oceans, and rivers.

2   But there is still no substitute for direct observation and laboratory analysis, and each spacecraft that has landed on the moon and returned to earth, manned or unmanned, has brought back information and samples of

The moon has neither an atmosphere nor surface water

the greatest value. The lack of a protective atmosphere and of running water to erode away surface features means that there is much to be learned on the moon about our common environment in space, both past and present. And from the composition and internal structure of the moon hints can be gleaned of its origin and past history, which may well bear upon those of the earth as well. Thus the study of the moon is also a part of the study of the earth, doubly justifying the effort of its exploration.

3   With the help of no more than binoculars it is easy to distinguish the two main kinds of lunar landscape, the dark, relatively smooth *maria* and the lighter, ruggedly mountainous highlands. Mare means "sea" in Latin, but the term is still used even though it has been known for a long time that these regions are not covered with water. The largest of the maria is Mare Imbrium, the Sea of Showers, which is over 1,000 km across. The maria are circular depressions covered with dark, loosely packed material—not solid rock. They are not perfectly smooth, but are marked by small craters, ridges, and cliffs. The available evidence indicates that maria consist of lava flows similar to basalt that have been broken up by meteorite impacts. It is curious and perhaps significant that nearly all the maria are on the lunar hemisphere that faces the earth.

4   The lunar highlands are scarred by innumerable craters ranging up to 236 km in diameter. Most of the craters are circular with raised rims that are steeper on the inside than on the outside, and some have mountain peaks at their centers. Certain craters, such as Tycho and Copernicus, have conspicuous streaks of light-colored matter radiating outward. These *rays* may extend for hundreds or thousands of kilometers, and seem to consist of lunar material sprayed outward. Craters resembling those on the moon are produced on the earth both by volcanic activity and by meteoric impact. There is no question that some of the lunar craters are of meteoric origin—after all, the moon cannot have avoided being struck by meteoroids in the past, and the slowness of geologic change there must have preserved the craters. However, present evidence points to a volcanic origin far in the past for the majority of the craters.

Mascons

5   A remarkable and wholly unexpected finding is that underneath some—but not all—of the maria are large, dense concentrations of mass—*mascons* for short. The presence of mascons was deduced from irregularities in the motions of artificial satellites set in orbit around the moon. When a satellite approached one of these maria, its speed increased, suggesting the presence of denser material whose gravitational pull is greater than that of the rest of the moon. To give an idea of the kind of object that could be responsible, calculations show that the gravitational anomaly near Mare Imbrium could be produced by a nickel-iron sphere 70 km in diameter whose center lies 50 km below the surface.

Maria are large, dark, smooth regions on the lunar surface that consist of lava pulverized by meteorites

Most lunar craters probably have volcanic origins

Mascons are dense bodies of matter under some maria

6	The first thought that comes to mind is that mascons are giant meteorites, the remains perhaps of asteroids that struck the moon long ago. The impact of such an asteroid would have produced a huge crater, which would later have filled in with debris and lava resulting from the collision to produce the maria of today. But this explanation does not seem altogether satisfactory. For one thing, it is hard to see why an asteroid colliding with the moon would not have shattered, even vaporized, at once. Another objection is that even if a nickel-iron meteorite of the required size were placed gently on the lunar surface, it would soon have migrated to the center of the moon by virtue of the pressure it would have exerted on the underlying material.

7	There is no lack of alternative possibilities. A plausible notion is that a mascon results from exceptionally dense lava that flowed into a large crater or into a porous part of the lunar crust and hardened there. A successful theory of mascons must account not only for their presence beneath certain maria but also for their absence from beneath others.

8	The mountains of the moon are thousands of meters high, which means that the moon's surface is about as irregular as the earth's. In order to support these irregularities, the moon must be quite rigid, which in view of the moon's size suggests that the lunar interior is nowhere near as hot as that of the earth. The existence of mascons is another argument for the rigidity of the moon. Even if they are thin layers of dense material rather than spherical lumps of iron, they cannot be resting on plastic rock like the asthenosphere of the earth or they would long ago have sunk far below where they are now.

The moon cannot have a plastic layer in its interior

The Mare Serenitatis is surrounded by highlands and mountains.

G. Check your understanding

1. Look at the first paragraph again. Are these statements correct or incorrect?

- Little was known about the moon's surface before the voyages of Apollo 11. ☐
- There are several reasons why we are sure the moon does not have much, if any, atmosphere. ☐

2. Look at paragraph 2 again. Is this statement correct or incorrect?

- The absence of an atmosphere and running water means that studies of the moon do not help to understand the earth. ☐

3. Look at paragraph 3 again. Are these statements correct or incorrect?

- The moon exhibits two principal features. ☐
- The 'seas' of the moon consist of solid rock. ☐
- The majority of the moon's 'seas' are on the side opposite the earth. ☐

4. Now look at paragraph 4 again. Are these statements correct or incorrect?

- Rays are a feature of most of the moon's craters. ☐
- Similar craters to those on the moon have been made by volcanoes on the earth. ☐
- Most craters on the moon have been caused by meteoroids. ☐

5. Now look at paragraph 5 again. Is this statement correct or incorrect?

- Satellites orbiting the moon retain a constant speed. ☐

6. Now look at paragraph 6 and say what these words refer to:

- line 2: that
- line 3: such
- line 3: which
- line 9: it
- line 10: it

7. Now look at paragraph 7 again. Is this statement correct or incorrect?

- The flow of dense lava is a possible reason for the existence of mascons. ☐

8. Now look at paragraph 8 again. Are these statements correct or incorrect?

- The moon is not as rigid as the earth. ☐
- The moon probably does not have an asthenosphere like the earth. ☐

H. Understanding discourse

Listen to a tutor giving some advice to a student shortly before his examinations. As you listen, note down the advice the tutor gives.

THE UNIVERSE

A. Understanding a printed text (1)

The following text will introduce you to the topic of the **Universe**. Look at the way it is divided into sections and paragraphs. Pay attention to the headings and notes in the margins, and to the illustration.

Now look at these questions:

1. The writer gives two reasons for studying the sun. What are they?

2. What are the main points of the first section?

3. What are the main points of the second section?

Read the passage through to find the answers to the questions. Remember, you do not have to understand every word to answer them.

THE SUN

1 The sun is the glorious body that dominates the solar system, and the origin and destiny of the earth as well as our daily lives are closely connected with solar phenomena. The astronomer has another reason for studying the sun closely, for it is in many ways a typical star. The properties of the sun that we can observe by virtue of its relative closeness, then, are interesting not only in themselves but also because they provide information about stars in general that would otherwise be inaccessible.

The sun is a typical star

Properties of the Sun

2   The sun is so large that 1,300,000 earths would fit into it. Like all other astronomical bodies, it is rotating, though with the peculiarity that its period of rotation is shorter near its equator than near its poles. Although conditions on the sun are very different from those on the earth, the basic matter of the two bodies appears to be the same. Even the relative amounts of different elements are similar, except for a vastly greater abundance of the lightest elements, hydrogen and helium, on the sun. At the low temperatures prevailing on the earth, most of the elements have combined to form compounds; in the hot sun the elements are usually present as individual atoms, most of them ionized.

Hydrogen and helium are extremely abundant in the sun

3   The surface temperature of the sun is about 5700°C. At this temperature all matter is gaseous, which means that the surface of the sun is a glowing gas envelope. Above the surface is a rapidly thinning atmosphere that consists principally of hydrogen, helium, and calcium. From this atmosphere great, flamelike *prominences* sometimes extend out into space, much like sheets of gas standing on their sides. During a total eclipse of the sun, when the moon obscures the sun's disk completely, a wide halo of pearly light can be seen around the dark moon. This halo, or *corona*, may extend out as much as a solar diameter and seems to have a great number of fine lines extending outward from the sun immersed in its general luminosity. The corona consists of ionized atoms and electrons in extremely rapid motion.

Solar prominences

The corona

4   Although the corona that we can see is relatively near the sun, indirect evidence indicates that, in very diffuse form, it also pervades much of the region between earth and sun. Most authorities even regard the sun's atmosphere as extending well beyond the earth's orbit—a radical change indeed from the older idea that interplanetary space is an all but total vacuum. The outward flow of ions and electrons in this atmosphere constitutes the solar wind which has been detected by rocket-borne instruments.

The solar wind

Sunspots

5   Marring the intense luminosity of the sun's surface at times are markings of reduced brightness called *sunspots*. Sunspots change continually in form, each one growing rapidly and then shrinking, with lifetimes of from 2 or 3 days to more than a month. The largest sunspots are many thousands of miles across, large enough to engulf several earths. Galileo, one of the first to study sunspots, noted that they moved across the sun's disk, evidence which he interpreted, as we do today, as indicating that the sun rotates on its axis. Sunspots appear black only because we see them against a brighter background; the blackest spots have temperatures of about 4200°C, sufficiently hot to glow brilliantly but nevertheless 1500°C cooler than the rest of the solar surface.

Sunspots appear dark only by comparison with the brighter solar surface around them

6   Sunspots generally appear in groups, each with a single large spot together with a number of smaller ones. Some groups contain as many as 80 separate spots. They tend to occur in two zones on either side of the solar equator and are rarely seen either near the equator or at latitudes on the sun higher than 35°. Sunspots seem to consist of gas that moves upward from the sun's interior, expanding and cooling as it spirals out. Strong magnetic fields are invariably associated with sunspots, and there is little doubt they are intimately related to the process of sunspot formation.

7   The number of spots on the sun changes with time. Approximately every 11 years the number of visible sunspots reaches a maximum, diminishing afterward so that 6 or 7 years later there are virtually no spots at all. Then the number increases to another maximum, and the *sunspot cycle*, as this periodic fluctuation is called, repeats itself.

The sunspot cycle is about 11 years long

8   The sunspot cycle has aroused much interest because a number of effects observable on the earth—such as disturbances in the terrestrial magnetic field (called *magnetic storms*), shortwave-radio fadeouts, changes in cosmic-ray intensity, and unusual auroral activity—follow this cycle, and there is evidence suggesting that some aspects of the weather do so also. There seem to be two different mechanisms responsible for events on the earth that are synchronized with sunspots:

Certain phenomena on earth follow the sunspot cycle

1 Intense bursts of ultraviolet light and x-rays are emitted from the sun more frequently during a sunspot maximum, which cause radio fadeouts by interacting with the ionosphere.

2 Vast streams of energetic protons and electrons shoot out of the sun from the vicinity of sunspot groups, and these streams cause magnetic storms and spectacular auroras and lead indirectly to variations in cosmic rays.

An active sunspot group photographed from a balloon-borne telescope at an altitude of 80,000 ft to avoid the distorting effects of atmospheric irregularities. The spots consist of relatively cool cores surrounded by filaments of outward-moving gases. The cellular background pattern arises from small-scale convection currents in the hot gases of the solar surface. Particle streams from this spot group produced magnetic disturbances and auroras on the earth.

B. Check your understanding

Now answer these questions:

1. What is unusual about the rotation of the sun?

2. In what major ways do the elements of the sun differ from those of the earth?

3. How does the writer describe the sun's surface?

4. What is a solar prominence?

5. What is a corona?

6. What is solar wind?

7. How would you describe a sunspot?

8. Where do sunspots occur?

9. What is the sunspot cycle?

10. What are the effects of the sunspot cycle on the earth?

C. Increase your vocabulary

1. Look at the first paragraph and say which words have the opposite meaning to:

- reachable
- is under the influence/authority of

2. Now look at paragraph 2 again. Can you explain the following?

- astronomical bodies
- peculiarity
- basic matter
- compound
- individual atoms

3. Now look at paragraph 3 and say which words have the same meaning as:

- put under the surface
- complete
- very narrow
- hides

4. Now look at paragraph 4 and say which words have the same meaning as:

- ·discovered the existence of
- scattered; spread out
- gets into every part of
- complete emptiness

5. Now look at paragraph 5 again. Can you explain the meaning of the following?

- marring
- engulf
- shrinking
- glow
- axis

6. Now look at paragraphs 6, 7 and 8 and say which words have the same meaning as the following:

- growing less
- always
- very closely
- almost
- happen at the same time
- neighbourhood

D. Check your grammar

PREPOSITIONS
Complete the following paragraphs using the right preposition:

Here _____ the earth, 93 million mi _____ the sun, a surface 1m^2 _____ area exposed _____ the vertical rays _____ the sun receives an average _____ nearly 20 kcal _____ energy/min. Adding _____ all the energy received _____ the earth's surface gives a staggering total, although this is but a tiny fraction _____ the sun's total radiation. And the sun has been emitting energy _____ this rate _____ billions of years. Where does it all come _____?

   We might be tempted to think _____ combustion, for fire is the only familiar natural source _____ energy that seems at all comparable _____ the sun. But a moment's reflection shows that the sun is *too* hot to burn; burning implies the combination _____ other elements _____ oxygen to form compounds, but _____ the sun nearly all compounds are decomposed _____ the terrific heat. And even if burning were physically possible, the heat obtainable _____ the best fuels known would be hopelessly inadequate to maintain the sun's temperature.

PARAGRAPH WRITING
Make complete sentences out of the following notes, putting the verbs in brackets in the right tense. Then arrange the sentences into one paragraph. Make sure that the paragraph makes sense, and that the sentences follow each other logically.

- the/part/galaxy/the/stars/Milky Way/all/of/our/of

  (*be*)

  _____

- analysing/the/scientists/to find out/starlight/nature/the/of/the/before/techniques/most/ physical/stars/of

  (*discover; not expect*)

  _____

- member/immense/stars/of/our/a/an/of/sun/aggregate

  (*be*)

  _____

- birth/evolution/we/its/star/trace/to/death/maturity/through/a/from/its/the/in fact/of

  (*be able to*)

  _____

- aggregates/universe/there/galaxies/and/many/the/in/these

  (*be; call*)

  _____

- we/deal/however/information/of/on/a/detailed/stars/of/thousands/great/today

  (*have*)

  _____

- others/vast/virtually/each/empty/the/by/reaches/space/from/of

  (*separate*)

  _____

- sun/the/other/even/telescope/to/a/of/light/point/powerful/star/no/most/the/than/more/ than/as

  (*appear*)

  _____

E. Understanding a lecture

Listen to this lecture on stars. Using the information the lecturer gives you, answer the questions below. The lecture is divided into sections. Listen to each section twice.

Section 1———————————————

- Is this statement correct or incorrect?

  There is enormous variety in the mass different stars contain. ☐

- How do stars compare in mass with the sun?

  _____

- The lecturer gives two major differences between stars. What are they?

  _____

  _____

- What are stars little bigger than the earth called?

  _____

- What is the diameter of the largest stars?

  _____

- The lecturer names one of the largest stars. Which is it?

  _____

Section 2———————————————

- Is this statement correct or incorrect?

  Antares has a density a thousand times that of sea-level air. ☐

- How much would 1 in^3 of a smaller star's substance weigh on the earth?

  _____

- Is this statement correct or incorrect?

  Electrons circle their nuclei at some distance in normal atoms. ☐

- If an atom collapses, what happens to the electrons and nuclei?

Section 3———————————————

- Note down the temperatures of:

  very hot stars

  _____

intermediate stars
_____

cooler stars
_____

● Note down the colours of the stars:

very hot stars
_____

Now listen to the lecture again and take notes. When you have done that, write a summary of the lecture. Your answers to the questions and your notes will help you.

intermediate stars
_____

cooler stars
_____

F. Understanding a printed text (2)

Read the following text carefully, looking up anything you do not understand.

Stellar Evolution

A body of matter with the mass and composition of a star must shine

1   A star shines because it is a large, compact aggregate of matter that contains abundant hydrogen. A body of this sort *cannot avoid* being luminous because of the energy liberated in the conversion of its hydrogen into helium. We may imagine as the starting point in a star's history a stage when its matter was an irregular mass of cool, diffuse gas and small, solid particles. Gravitation in such a mass would concentrate it into a smaller space. The gradual contraction would heat the gas, much as the gas in a tire pump is heated by compression. At length the temperature would grow high enough for hydrogen to be converted into helium, and the mass would begin to glow brightly. From this time on the tendency to contract would be counterbalanced by the pressure of radiation from the hot interior, so shrinking would stop and the star would maintain a nearly constant size. The diameter of a star is thus determined by an equilibrium between gravitational forces pulling its material inward and forces due to radiation pushing its material outward.

2   A star does not shine because some occult force has started it shining; it shines because it has a certain mass and a certain composition. If we could somehow build a star by heaping together sufficient matter of the right composition, it would start to shine of its own accord.

3   A star consumes its hydrogen rapidly if it is large, slowly if it is small. A fairly small star like our sun makes its supply of hydrogen last for a period of the order of 10 billion years; probably the sun is now about halfway through this part of its career. When the hydrogen supply at last begins to run low in a star like the sun, the life of the star is by no means ended but enters its most spectacular phase. Further gravitational contraction makes the interior still hotter, and other nuclear reactions become possible—particularly reactions in which atoms of heavier elements are made by a combination of helium atoms. These reactions, once started, give out so much energy that the star expands to become a giant. Energy is now being poured out at a prodigious rate, so the star's life as a giant is much shorter than the earlier part of its existence.

Stars expand as they grow old

▼

4   Eventually the new energy-producing reactions run out of fuel, and again the star shrinks—although probably not without a few last brief flare-ups, which we see from the earth as *novae* ("new stars") that shine brilliantly for a week or two and then subside into insignificance. The shrinking ultimately reduces the star to the white dwarf state. As a slowly contracting dwarf the star may remain luminous for billions of years more with its energy now coming from the contraction, from nuclear reactions involving elements heavier than helium, and from proton-proton reactions in a very thin outer atmosphere of hydrogen.

White dwarfs are very old stars

5   Stars much more massive than the sun have somewhat different histories. Eventually they become unstable and explode violently, emitting enormous amounts of material. Such explosions we observe as *supernovae,* flare-ups 10,000 or more times as luminous as ordinary novae. Having lost perhaps half its mass, a star of this kind can then subside like its smaller brethren into a dwarf star.

Supernovae

6   Today astronomers believe that the residual dwarfs of supernovae are different from ordinary white dwarfs because of the large mass of their parent stars. These hypothetical dwarfs are calculated to have densities far in excess of ordinary dwarfs, with masses comparable to that of the sun packed into spheres perhaps 15 km (9 mi) in diameter. The matter of such a star would weigh billions of tons per cubic inch. (If the earth were this dense, it would fit into a large apartment house.) Under the pressures that would be present the most stable form of matter is the neutron. *Pulsars*, which emit brief, intense bursts of radio waves at regular intervals, are believed to be rotating neutron stars with magnetic fields that lead to radio emission in narrow beams; as a pulsar rotates, its beams swing with it to produce the observed fluctuations. A notable pulsar is located at the center of the Crab nebula, which is the remnant of a supernova that was seen in A.D. 1054 and has been expanding and glowing brightly ever since.

Pulsars are believed to be neutron stars

Spiral Galaxies

7   The great band of misty light called the Milky Way forms a continuous ring around the heavens. When it is examined with a telescope, the Milky Way is an unforgettable sight. Instead of a dim glow we now see countless individual stars, stars as thick as the sand grains on a beach although so faint and far away that the naked eye cannot distinguish them. In other parts of the sky the telescope reveals many stars not visible to the eye, but nowhere else in such profusion. Clearly the stars are not uniformly distributed in space—a simple observation which has profound implications concerning the structure and evolution of the universe.

The galaxy of which the sun is a member appears in the sky as the Milky Way

8   The appearance of the Milky Way tells us something about the arrangement of stars in our galaxy: most of them are concentrated in a relatively thin disklike region, with the sun located near the central plane of the disk. When we look along the plane of the disk, we see a dense mass of stars (the Milky Way), and when we look toward the top or bottom of the disk, we see fewer stars. Careful study shows that the disk of stars has a thicker central nucleus, so that it is shaped something like a fried egg (Fig. 13.3). The disk is about 100,000 light-years in diameter and the stars in it are chiefly located in two spiral arms that extend from the nucleus. The sun is about 30,000 light-years from the center of the galaxy. (The *light-year* is a unit of length in astronomy equal to the distance light travels in a year; since the speed of light is 300,000 km/s, a light-year is about 9.5 million million km long.)

9   The stars of the galaxy are all revolving about its center, which is what they must do if the galaxy is not to gradually collapse because of the gravitational attraction of its parts. (The planets do not fall into the sun because of their similar orbital motion.)

10   Associated with our galaxy are a number of huge globular clusters of stars that form a sort of halo or corona around the central disk. Thus the true form of the galaxy as a whole is roughly spherical. The stars in the spiral arms are of different ages, including very young ones still in the process of formation; those in the rest of the galaxy are all very old. Presumably all the matter of the galaxy was originally a spherical cloud of gas and dust that gradually concentrated in the spiral arms, leaving behind those stars that had already come into being. New stars continued to form from the gas and dust in the spiral arms, which is why the stars there are of all ages.

11   All the stars in the universe are members of galaxies, many of which are spiral galaxies that closely resemble our own in size and shape. Some, however, lack a central disk of spiral arms, and consist simply of very old stars like the ones in the globular clusters of our galaxy.

12   Thus we are able to picture the universe as made up of galaxies of stars, each one isolated in space and separated from its nearest neighbors by distances of a million light-years or more. In all directions, in unbroken succession, these galaxies extend to the farthest parts of the universe that our instruments can penetrate. Not only is the earth an undistinguished planet circling an undistinguished star; even the great galaxy that includes the sun is no different from millions of others.

13   Through all this vast array of uncounted suns and unimaginable distances runs a uniformity of material and structural pattern. The elements of the earth are the elements of the spiral galaxies, the sun generates energy by a process repeated in billions of other stars, and the form of our galaxy recurs again and again in the rest of the universe. Everywhere we find the same ultimate particles of matter, the same kinds of energy, the same patterns of structure. We can study at firsthand no more than a tiny fragment of the universe, yet so consistent is the whole that from this fragment we can extend our knowledge wherever our instruments enable us to see.

A mosaic of several photographs of the Milky Way between the constellations Sagittarius and Cassiopeia.

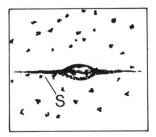

Fig. 13.3 Cross-sectional sketch of our galaxy. Globular clusters are shown as patches, and the sun is located at S. The diameter of the galaxy is about 100,000 light-years.

G. Check your understanding

1. Look at the first paragraph again. Are these statements correct or incorrect?

- Stars begin in a small space. ☐
- Hydrogen is converted into helium at low temperatures. ☐
- A star continues to grow smaller throughout its history. ☐

2. Now look at paragraph 2 again. Is this statement correct or incorrect?

- Mass and composition are what make stars luminous. ☐

3. Now look at paragraph 3 again. Are these statements correct or incorrect?

- A star maintains a constant level of hydrogen. ☐
- Nuclear reactions lead to the expansion of a star. ☐

4. Now look at paragraph 4 again. Are these statements correct or incorrect?

- Novae are not really new stars. ☐
- There are no nuclear reactions in a star in the white dwarf state. ☐

5. Now look at paragraph 5 again. Is this statement correct or incorrect?

- Supernovae emit the same amount of light as novae. ☐

6. Now look at paragraph 6 again. Are these statements correct or incorrect?

- The remains of supernovae have a greater density than white dwarfs. ☐
- Can you explain the term *pulsar* in your own words?

7. Now look at paragraph 7 again. Are these statements correct or incorrect?

- The Milky Way contains the greatest number of stars. ☐
- Stars are spread out evenly throughout the universe. ☐

8. Now look at paragraph 8 again. Using Fig. 13.3, explain what this paragraph is about.

9. Now look at paragraph 9 again.

- Why does the galaxy not collapse?

10. Now look at paragraph 10 again. Are these statements correct or incorrect?

- It is not known what shape the galaxy has. ☐
- All stars were created at the same time. ☐

11. Now look at paragraph 11 again. Is this statement correct or incorrect?

- Not all galaxies are the same shape. ☐

12. Now look at paragraph 12 again. Is this statement correct or incorrect?

- Our galaxy is totally different from all other galaxies. ☐

13. Now look at paragraph 13 again. Are these statements correct or incorrect?

- The earth shares the same elements as the stars. ☐
- Our instruments cannot reach more than a small part of the universe. ☐

H. Understanding discourse

Listen to a tutor giving some advice on how to prepare for examinations. Note down the advice he gives.